# A Quilted Christmas

## Complete Directions for 34 Holiday Gifts

Edited by Bonnie Browning

American Quilter's Society

P. O. Box 3290 • Paducah, KY 42002-3290

The American Quilter's Society (AQS) is dedicated to promoting the accomplishments of today's quilters. Located in Paducah, Kentucky, AQS publishes books and sponsors events to honor quiltmakers and their work, as well as help to cultivate their creativity and innovation.

**Library of Congress Cataloging-in-Publication Data**

A quilted Christmas / edited by Bonnie Browning.
     p.     cm.
ISBN 0-89145-863-8
1. Patchwork--Patterns.  2. Machine appliqué--Patterns.
3. Machine quilting.  4. Christmas decorations.  I. Browning, Bonnie,    1944-  .
TT835.Q5355   1995
745.594' 12--dc20            95-35797
                     CIP

The editor and authors have provided the information and patterns in this book in good faith. The American Quilter's Society has no control of materials or methods used, and therefore assumes no responsiblity for the use of or results obtained from this information.

Additional copies of this book may be ordered from:

**American Quilter's Society**
P.O. Box 3290
Paducah, KY 42002-3290
@$18.95. Add $2.00 for postage and handling.

Copyright: 1995, AQS

Printed by IMAGE GRAPHICS, INC., Paducah, Kentucky

# Acknowledgments

C & A Christmas Exchange, Grand Rivers, KY; and
Martha Hinton, Kuttawa, KY, for loaning Christmas items
for the cover photo.

William E. Schroeder for modeling the boy's vest.

All the AQS authors who provided new projects to help
make this book a reality.

The AQS staff who worked diligently to produce our first
Christmas book: Marcie Hinton, editorial assistant; Charles
R. Lynch, photographer; Terry Williams, cover and art
designer; Whitney Hopkins, illustrator designer; Lanette
Ballard, layout designer; and Laurie Swick, proofreader.

# Introduction

If you make gifts for your family and friends, you will enjoy
making these wonderful quilted designs from well-known
AQS authors to enrich your holiday celebrations. Thirty-four
authors developed new projects to give you an opportunity to
try a variety of techniques.

For those of you who enjoy appliqué, you'll find projects
using needle turn, channel, 3-dimensional, and fusible
appliqué. Machine aficionados will enjoy strip piecing, spin-
ning lace by machine, straight stitch machine appliqué, and
paper foundation piecing. Whether you are a beginning or
expert quilter, there are great gift ideas for everyone.

Each project has a materials list, cutting instructions, assembly diagrams, step-by-step instructions, and patterns. You
can use your favorite method to piece, appliqué, quilt, and
finish these projects.

We hope you have fun making your gifts this year. All of
the AQS authors and staff wish you **A Quilted Christmas**!

Bonnie Browning
Editor

# Angelic Lace

### by Sharee Dawn Roberts

She's beautiful, she's precious, she's waiting to spring to life beneath the needle of your sewing machine in lacy glory. She might float above your tree top or stand sweetly on a shelf; but she is sure to delight all who admire her opalescent gown and heavenly wings!

## FEATURED TECHNIQUES
## Spinning lace by machine

## MATERIALS LIST

⅔ yds. "Sulky Solvy" (24" x 20")
One 1½" styrofoam ball
14" x 6" piece fusible vinyl
Gold star garland (for halo)
Gold ribbon (to tie around neck)
Fray Stoppa
Teflon Pressing Sheet
Glue gun with "cool temperature" glue sticks
Pearl cotton or string (for tying)
Metafil needle, size 80/12
Single groove cording foot

## SPECIALTY THREADS

Mokuba Jewelry Yarn, silver (couching cord to trim wings and gown)
Madeira Estaz #01 (for angel's hair)
Sulky 30 wt. Rayon machine embroidery thread, color 1071
Madeira Dazzle Metallic thread, color 380
Thread, color 301
Sulky Sliver color #8024
YLI Pearl Crown Rayon color #401
Kreinik Ombre color #3200

Sharee Dawn Roberts, Paducah, KY, is internationally known for her high fashion quilted clothing and special machine art techniques. She is the author of **Creative Machine Art**, AQS, and owns Web of Thread in Paducah. Sharee has been a designer for the Fairfield Fashion Show, and won the grand prize in 1987 and 1988 at the AQS/Hobbs Fashion Show. Her clothing has been shown in galleries and exhibitions throughout the U.S., Japan, and Europe.

Sharee Dawn Roberts

## INSTRUCTIONS

•First, we want to "spin" the lace for our pretty little angel. If you have never stitched machine lace before, you will love this technique that creates the most gorgeous lace to use in clothing and crafts. With a little experience, you will master lace-making by machine and think of all kinds of projects to use your lace.

•Start with your piece of water soluble stabilizer and spread it flat on a work surface. Use a wide assortment of pretty threads (include all of the threads listed under "Specialty Threads") to create a collage on top of half of the stabilizer, pulling long 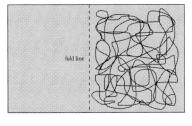 strands from the spools and arranging the threads on top of the Solvy. Do not layer the threads too thickly, but try to cover most of your work area with a good mixture.

•Now fold over the stabilizer to trap the threads between the two layers. The next step is a little unconventional, and you will wonder if the directions are printed correctly. Use a medium hot dry iron to fuse the stabilizer together and you will have a sandwich with the pretty threads in between. You will just have to trust me; the Solvy will not melt nor stick to your iron! What does happen, is the layers of Solvy stick to each other, fusing the thread package into a single sheet with the loose threads trapped firmly in between. But do be careful that no steam escapes from your iron, or the Solvy will start to dissolve.

•Next, stitch a grid to connect all of the threads, so that when you wash away the stabilizer, the collage of threads will hold together. Fill your bobbin with the 30 wt. Sulky Rayon and use a Metafil needle and the Madeira Dazzle on top. Start stitching at one corner and sew long lines all the

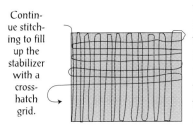

Continue stitching to fill up the stabilizer with a crosshatch grid.

way to the bottom, pivot, and return back to the top with the lines spaced approximately ½" apart. After you have completed the vertical lines, repeat the same sequence, with horizontal lines spaced ½" apart. It is somewhat boring sewing, but relaxing also. (Certainly easy, huh?)

•After your stabilizer is filled with a nice grid to connect all of the threads, it is time for the fun part! Take your collage to the sink to wash away all of the stabilizer, gently rubbing together to help wash it completely away. Isn't it amazing? You have created the most beautiful custom lace imaginable. Carefully press your lace dry.

•Now cut the pattern pieces from newsprint and pin them onto the lace. With the Sulky rayon in the top and the bobbin, set your sewing machine for medium-wide zigzag and use the single-groove cording foot. Center the silver yarn underneath the cording foot, and use the cut edge of the pattern pieces as a guide. Couch along the bottom curve of the angel's body, stopping at the straight line. Couch all

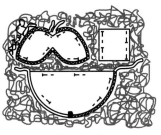

Diagram A

the way around the wings; (diagram A) run a thin line of "Fray Stoppa" all the way along the couching lines. After it is dry, cut around the pattern pieces, trimming right next to the silver yarn on any edge that has been couched.

•You now have three pieces of lace to form your angel. For the gown, protect your ironing surface with the teflon sheet and fuse the piece of fusible vinyl to the lace following the manufacturer's instructions, then trim the vinyl among the outside edges of your lace.

Lace to wrap styrofoam ball for the head.

•The rest is easy, and all accomplished with a glue gun! Shape the body into a cone, overlapping the back seam until the gown is the size and shape you want, and glue the back seam together. Tightly wrap the styrofoam ball with the scrap of lace and tie it at the bottom with the pearl cotton. Snip the tip of the cone so that the gathered end of the styrofoam ball can slip inside the "neck" and add a little glue to hold the head secure. Wind the "Estaz" in coils around the top of the angel's head and tack it in place with the tip of the glue gun.

•Bend the gold star garland in a small circle to fashion her halo, with a 3" stem to stick inside the styrofoam ball to hold it in place at the back of the angels head. (Diagram B). Tie a ribbon around her neck with the gold ribbon.

•Last of all, run a thin line of glue with the tip of your glue gun along line "A" of the wings and gently press them onto the back of your angel. Your beautiful angel will be so graceful, you will believe she's ready to fly away!

Lace for the wings, couched all the way around the silver yarn.

Lace for body, couched around the bottom curved edge with the silver yarn.

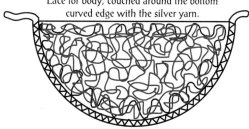

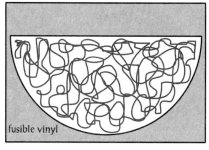

fusible vinyl

Fuse, then trim along edge of lace.

Tie

Tuck inside "neck."

Diagram B

Line A

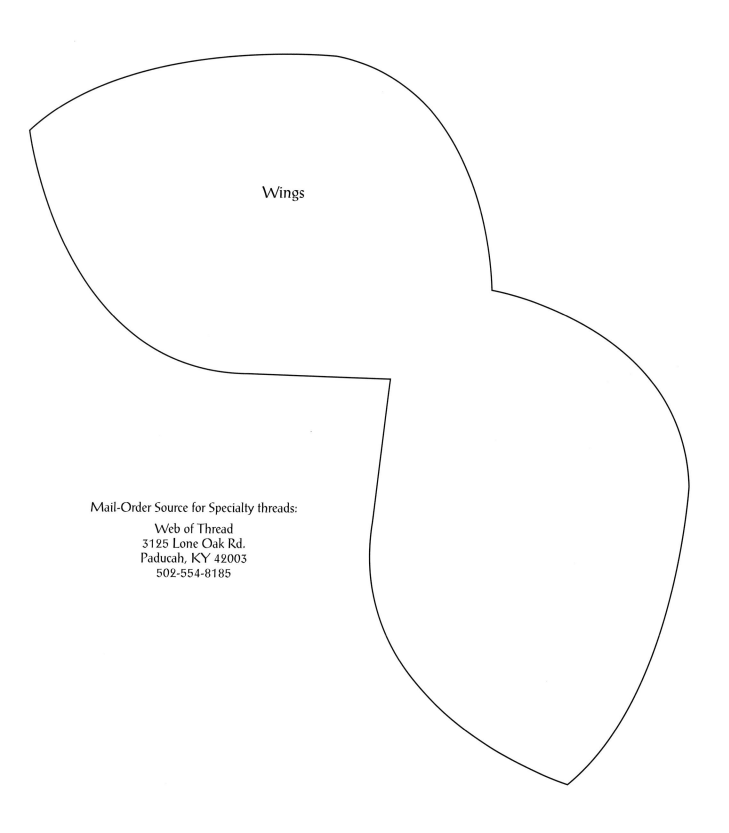

Wings

Mail-Order Source for Specialty threads:

Web of Thread
3125 Lone Oak Rd.
Paducah, KY 42003
502-554-8185

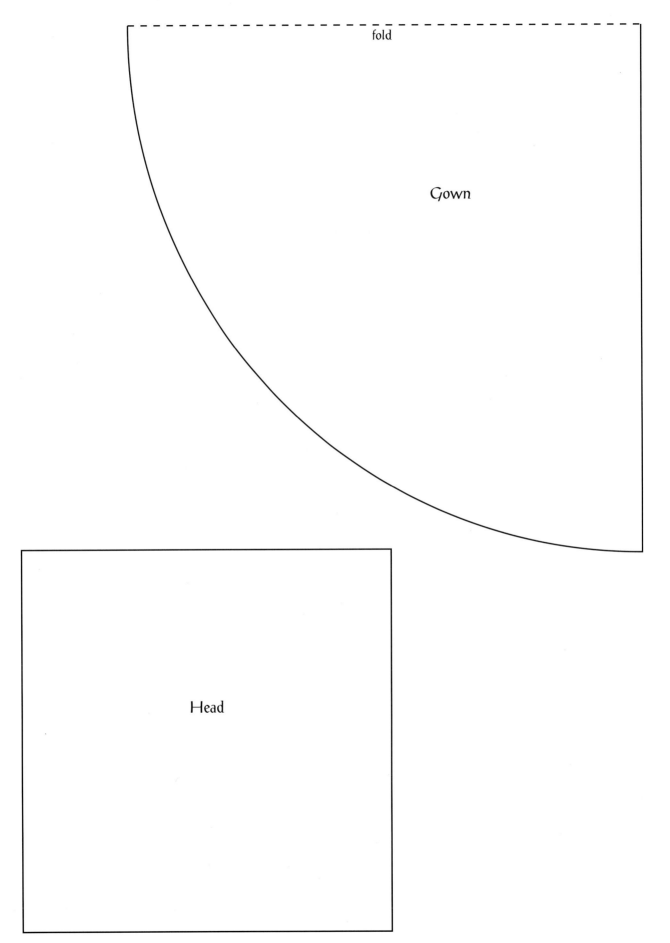

fold

Gown

Head

10

# BIRDS AND BOWS
## CHRISTMAS TREE SKIRT

**by Letty Martin**

Appliqué and piecing combine to create this festive 50" diameter Christmas tree skirt. Straight stitch machine appliqué the swags, birds, and bows, and your tree skirt will be done in a jiffy. A wonderful gift to yourself or a special friend.

### FEATURED TECHNIQUES
Machine piecing
Straight stitch machine appliqué

## MATERIALS LIST

16 - ¼ yd. pcs. of greens; lights, medium, and darks
¼ yd. red print for cardinals
⅛ yd. black for mask on cardinal
⅛ yd. gold for bows
⅝ yd. red and green plaid for swags
4 yds. white on white or muslin for outer edge of skirt, backing, and binding
54" x 54" square of cotton quilt batt
6 – ¼" black doll buttons for cardinal eyes

## OTHER SUPPLIES

Template plastic
Freezer paper
Transparent nylon thread, smoke and clear
Sewing thread, colors to match appliqué fabric
Sewing machine and appliqué foot
General sewing supplies
Starch or sizing
Small measuring cup
Cotton swabs

Letty Martin, Lake Orion, MI, is the author of **Straight Stitch Machine Appliqué: History, Patterns & Instructions for This Easy Technique**, AQS. This book is the result of her love of sewing and quiltmaking. Teaching at quilt shops and giving workshops to quilt guilds on how to use this technique keeps her busy.

Letty Martin

## CUTTING GUIDE

54 A, light, medium & dark greens
54 AR, different light, medium & dark greens
12 B  Swags
6 C  Cardinal masks
6 1" gold square  for bird beak
6 D  Cardinals
5 E  Bows
1 F  Half bow
1 G  Half bow
6 H  Bow tails
6 I  Bow tails
6 J Tree skirt bottoms
5 yds. 2" wide bias for binding

## INSTRUCTIONS

•Make a plastic template of triangle A.

•Two sets of templates will be needed for the appliqué. One set will be cut from template plastic and used to cut out the fabric shapes of the appliqué design. The second set is cut from freezer paper. Place the template plastic over the patterns B through I. Carefully trace, label, and cut out each piece. Using the plastic templates you have already made, trace around B, for example, on the paper side of the freezer paper. Cut two to four other pieces of freezer paper large enough to fit piece B. Stack, paper side up, pin, and cut out. Each freezer paper template can be used two to four times, or until its edges get bent over and it is no longer an accurate shape. The freezer paper templates are used in preparing the fabric appliqué pieces for straight stitch machine appliqué. Cut freezer paper templates for B through I.

•To make the fabric appliqué pieces, trace around plas-

tic template on the wrong side of the fabric. Cut out with a ³⁄₁₆" seam allowance. You can cut several layers of fabric at one time as you do not need the traced appliqué shape on each piece. Refer to the Cutting Guide for the amount of each template piece needed.

•To prepare a piece for appliqué, center a freezer paper template, shiny side facing you on the wrong side of the same shape fabric piece (template label goes on the wrong side of fabric). Using the tip and edge of the iron, press the fabric seam allowance back over the freezer paper. The edge of the freezer paper makes a natural fold line for the fabric. To help retain a nice crisp fold, paint the seam allowance with some starch or sizing. Pour or spray starch into a small measuring cup and dip cotton swab into starch, then roll it around the edge of the cup to remove excess starch. Paint it on the seam allowance, and press again. Corners and curved areas especially need this treatment to keep the seams turned under once the freezer paper template is removed and the fabric piece pinned in place ready to be straight stitch machine appliquéd.

•Corners may be pressed in two ways depending how pointed they are. Right angle corners can be handled by pressing each side in making sure the seams are all on the back of the appliqué piece. Pointed points need a mitered fold (Figure 1). First press over the seam allowance at the tip, then press in each side creating a

fabric

freezer
paper

Figure 1, Mitering points

mitered fold. Seam allowance may need to be trimmed some to reduce bulk at the tip of these points.

•Inner curves will need to be clipped to within two or three threads of the fold line. Outer curves will not need to be clipped. However, if your seam allowance is more than ³⁄₁₆", trimming may be necessary. Too small or too large of a seam allowance each present their own problems.

•Those edges of an appliqué piece covered by another piece do not need to be turned under.

•Pin prepared appliqué pieces in place. Put pins in the middle of the piece. To straight stitch machine appliqué you will be sewing very close to the edge of the appliqué using the straight stitch. Sew slowly. Drop needle at corners and pivot.

•To get your sewing machine ready for appliqué, wind bobbins to match the colors of your appliqué fabrics. Use transparent nylon as the upper thread. Use clear for light to medium colors and smoke for medium to dark colors. Loosen your tension. Use the appliqué foot and set stitch length about 2.5 or 10 to 12 stitches per inch. Bobbin thread color should match the color of the appliqué piece. Change bobbins as necessary. Secure ends of thread when necessary by back stitching with a shorter stitch length. Only those shapes you stitch all the way around, such as the cardinal, need to be secured.

## CONSTRUCTION

•The tree skirt is made in six sections. The inner part of the tree skirt is made of pieced rectangles. Using the eight colors you cut with A, piece three rectangles. Place two A's right side together, off setting enough so it is ¼" to the raw edge you will sew along. Measure and trim each rectangle to 3⁷⁄₁₆"x 5½" (Figure 2). Sew three rectangles with the Ar's. Notice the angles go in different directions in the A and Ar's. Using three rectangles made with

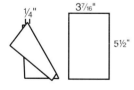

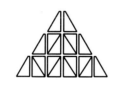

Figure 2                    Figure 3

each A and Ar, arrange as shown (Figure 3).

•Add individual triangles to the ends of each row to complete the pieced section. Two colors will need to be repeated. Use all of the colors in each section but place them in

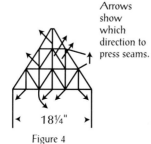

Arrows show which direction to press seams.

18¼"

Figure 4

different positions. Sew the pieces together in each row, then sew the rows together. Each rectangle is a finished size of 2¹⁵⁄₁₆" x  5". The bottom raw edge of the pieced rectangle unit will be 18¼". Sew six pieced rectangle units. Press as shown in Figure 4.

•Make a master pattern for tree skirt bottoms by tracing template J-a. Lay freezer paper over template J-b, matching lower edge marked A. continue tracing the lower arc; extend the top edge of J-b 4" to complete pattern. Place pattern on folded fabric; cut six.

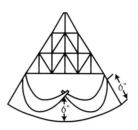

Figure 5

•Sew a white tree skirt bottom to a green pieced rectangle unit. Looking at Figure 5, position two prepared swags on the white tree skirt bottom. Where the ends of the swags cross and meet at the side seam allowance they will be 6" from the bottom of the white section. Straight stitch machine appliqué the swags in place.

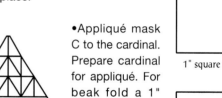

Figure 6
Folding squares to make beak

1" square

•Appliqué mask C to the cardinal. Prepare cardinal for appliqué. For beak fold a 1" square of gold fabric as shown in Figure 6. Press. Pin cardinal in place, slip beak under bird and appliqué (Fig. 7). Repeat six times.

Figure 7

•Sew two sections together. Where swags meet, appliqué a full bow. Appliqué tails first, I, H, then E. Repeat sewing two sections together and appliqué bow. The remaining two pieces will be left open to place skirt around tree. Sew a tail I and half bow F to one edge, and tail H and half bow G to the other section. Join sections, leaving the seam with the half bows open. Sew on buttons for bird eyes.

Wrong side turn over

Cut out 1" larger than tree skirt.

•Cut a 1½ yard length of backing fabric. Cut off selvage. Also cut a 11" x 45" section. Fold each piece in half lengthwise to find the centers, crease.

1½ yds        11" x 45"

Matching centers, pin and sew together. Backing is now large enough to fit the tree skirt.

•On a large flat surface, layer in the following order: batt, backing right side up, and the tree skirt wrong side up. Smooth out and pin to secure. Cut out around top one inch larger.

•To make center hole to allow skirt to fit around tree; cut out a template of center hole, 2" for an artificial tree or 2¼" for a real tree. Place over center of tree skirt and trace around the template. This is your sewing line. Sew up one open edge, around center hole and down the other side with a ¼" seam. Cut through batt and backing, between open edges of tree skirt around center hole. Clip seam in center. Turn right side out.

•Smooth all layers from the center out. Pin baste and quilt. Quilt pieced section as shown in drawing. Quilt next to the appliqué pieces.

•Sew a line of basting in the seam allowance at the edge of the skirt. Trim away the batt and backing even with the tree skirt.

•Cut 2" wide strips of bias, joining a total of 5 yards. Fold in half lengthwise and sew to edge of tree skirt on the

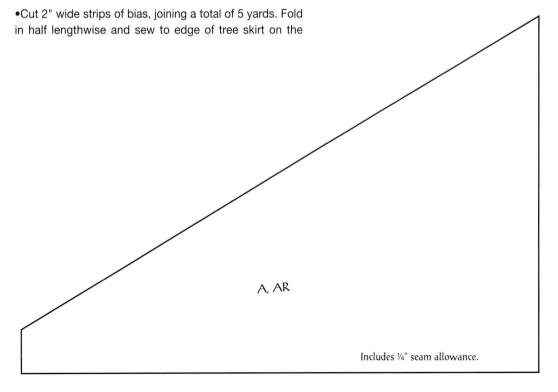

A, AR

Includes ¼" seam allowance.

# BIRDS AND BOWS

Finished sizes of pieces are shown; seam allowances will be added when fabric pieces are cut out.

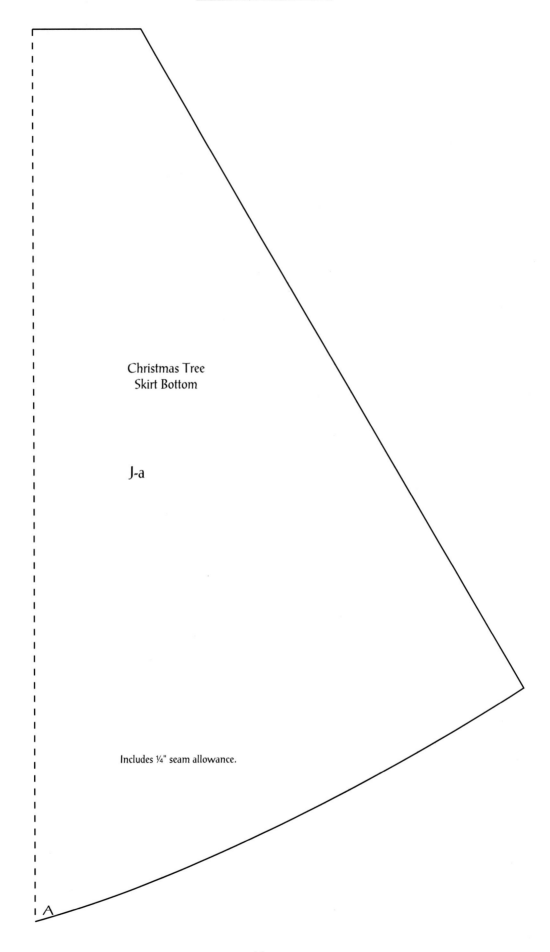

Christmas Tree
Skirt Bottom

J-a

Includes ¼" seam allowance.

A

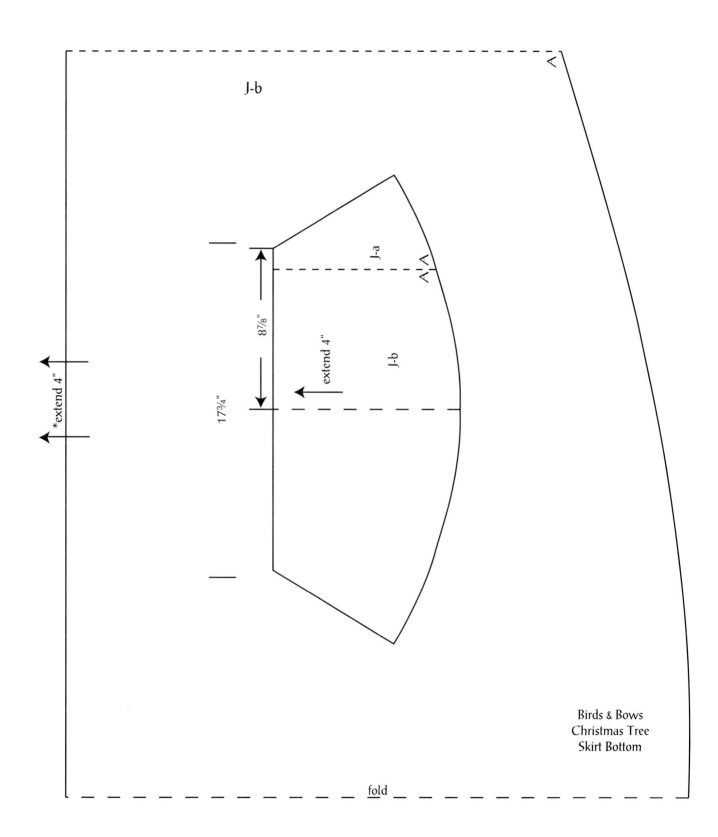

J-b

J-a

A-A

A

J-b

8⅞"

17¾"

extend 4"

*extend 4"

Birds & Bows
Christmas Tree
Skirt Bottom

fold

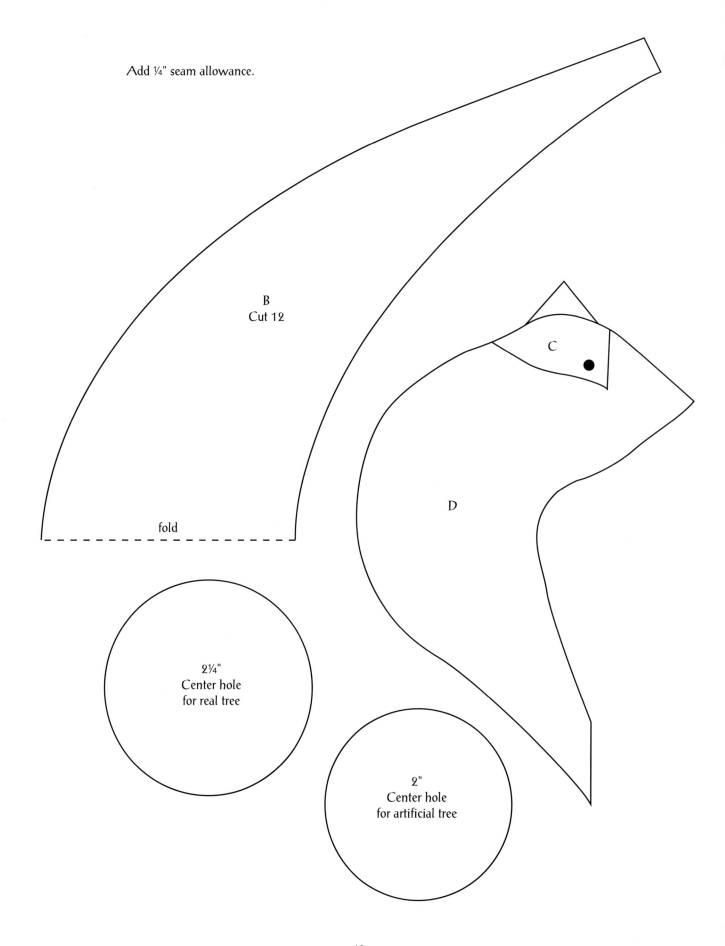

Add ¼" seam allowance.

B
Cut 12

C

D

fold

2¼"
Center hole
for real tree

2"
Center hole
for artificial tree

# BLUE SPRUCE
## WALLHANGING

### by Gwen Marston

In a time when Christmas has become increasingly commercial, this 18" x 20" quilt is an elegant and quiet way to say "Peace on Earth." Blue spruce is one in a series of twelve minimal quilts. The principal is that in some cases, less is more. Here, less piecing, less color, and more quilting combine to make a statement about simplicity and purity of design. Closely woven, fine white cotton is the background for the cobalt blue Christmas tree.

## FEATURED TECHNIQUES
## Machine piecing
## Hand quilted feathers

## MATERIALS LIST

1 - 4" square blue 100% cotton fabric
½ yd. white 100% cotton fabric

## INSTRUCTIONS

•Add ¼" seam allowance to the pattern pieces and cut the tree shapes. Piece the tree section of the quilt.

•Cut the side pieces in the tree strip. Cut them longer than needed, about 10", and trim them off later. Join them to the tree and press.

•Cut the top section of the quilt 3⅓" x 18".

•Cut the bottom of the quilt 18" x 14¼".

•Center the tree and join all three sections of the quilt. Press, and square it up with a rotary cutter.

•A silver pencil was used for marking this quilt. The quilting design has been supplied. Lay this pattern under your top and trace the design. It may be necessary to adjust it slightly so the feathers don't bump into each other.

•The quilt is finished with a single binding, cut on the straight of grain.

Gwen Marston, Beaver Island, MI, is a professional quiltmaker, author, and teacher who has written twelve books, and produced a series of videos on quilt-making. She has taught quilting and exhibited her quilts across the United States and abroad. Gwen is well known for teaching quilters to have fun in their quilting. Drafting feathers is one of her specialties that was published in **Quilting with Style: Principles for Great Pattern Design**, AQS. Her next book, **Liberated Quiltmaking**, will be published by AQS in 1996.

Gwen Marston

## Blue Spruce – pattern

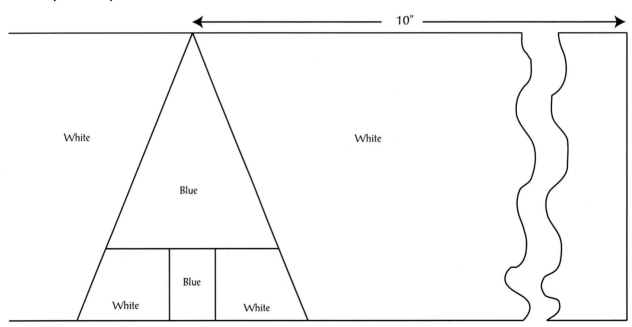

# BLUE SPRUCE

# BOUQUET OF ROSES
## WALLHANGING

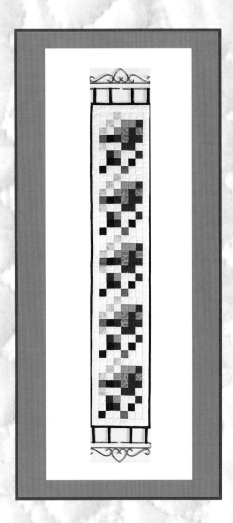

**by Joyce Peaden**
A small segment of an Anne Orr bouquet, complement-ed by an innovative support structure, makes a repeti-tive design for a long, thin bellpull. Anne Orr was an early twentieth century needlework artist, who pub-lished fanciful piecing patterns which were similar to her own cross stitch designs, using one-half to three-quarter inch squares of fabric in place of crossed stitches. This bellpull is Joyce Peaden's interpretation of Anne Orr-type designs.

## FEATURED TECHNIQUES
### Strip piecing

## MATERIALS LIST

¼ yd. each of red, plain coral, print coral, pink, and light green
½ yd. dark green for strips and binding
1 yd. white for strips, unpieced borders, and backing

## INSTRUCTIONS

•This bell pull (6½" x 32½") is accomplished by strip piecing according to pattern. The finesse is achieved by cutting the strips on the *lengthwise grain* and accurate machine stitching with a fine needle.

•Note that there are five equal "repeats" in the work, each of which is comparable to a quilt block, except that it is rectangular.

•Each unit has 48 pieces: 10 red, 3 print coral, 4 plain coral, 4 pink, 4 dark green, 2 light green, and 21 white. A strip is cut for each piece in the repeat unit. Each strip will be five times the length of each unfinished piece, plus a little leeway. Example: unfinished side of square

Joyce Peaden, Prosser, WA, pieced her first quilt, "Devil's Claw," as a distraction to the Battle of Iwo Jima in 1945. She began serious piecing again in the mid-1970's. Joyce has authored research papers on "Donated Quilts Warmed Wartorn Europe" and "The Multicolored Geometric Pieced Sails of Mindano," published by the American Quilt Study Group. Her book, **Irish Chain Quilts: A Workbook of Irish Chain and Related Patterns**, was published by AQS.

Joyce Peaden

is 1¼ inches; number of pieced units totals 5.
1¼" x 5 = 6 ¼" + 1 = 7 ¼".

•Cut 10 red strips on the lengthwise grain of the fabric, and continue by cutting strips of each color according to number as indicated.

•Compose and sew each row in order, by following the picture. The first row will be white, white, pink, white, white, white. The second row will be white, pink, white, plain coral, plain coral, red. Continue with rows 3 through 8.

•Press rows in alternate directions, after all sewing is completed.

•Crosscut in same width as original strip, or 1¼", and keep in order on a tray.

•Sew rows 1 and 2 together in chain fashion.

| | | dark green |
|---|---|---|
| | | light green |
| | | red |
| | | plain coral |
| | | print coral |
| | | pink |
| | | white |

•Add row 3, and continue with rows 4 through 8.

•Repeat design making five rectangular blocks.

•Combine the five repeats.

•Press seams upward when entire bellpull unit is sewn together. Finger press seams first. Be very careful not to distort the work while pressing.

•Lay the work out lengthwise on the ironing board, making sure it is straight, with the seams turned upward, pinning at the edge if necessary. Press with a steam iron, using a downward motion only, and just lightly touching the unit. This is not blocking, but holding, as sewn.

•The work will be very flexible at this point, but is stabilized by the borders. Lay the piece out on a padded table, and the border down on it as it falls, making sure exactly the same length of border is used on each long side, and then each short side. Pin and sew. Miter corners. Assemble with backing and very thin batting. Quilt.

•Apply binding, using a 1" wide strip for a ¼" binding. Bias binding is my favorite, but straight binding is fine on a wallhanging that does not get a lot of wear. Corners with inside construction are shown, but binding with butted ends would be equally good on this small piece of work. Finish to the front of the work, so that the stitches will pucker the fabric to match the quilting.

•This format will be good for your own innovative Anne Orr-type pattern. Five or seven strips may also be used and the strips may be ½"or 1" wide finished. Many strips complicate the construction, and this project was planned to be fun. Try ethnic cross stitch variations, or motifs from hardanger patterns.

# CANDY CANE EXPRESS
## CHILD'S VEST

**by Alexandra Capadalis Dupré**

Every child on your Christmas list will want a Candy Cane Express vest. They'll be surprised that the candy cane and gingerbread man in the pocket are toys. The gingerbread man makes a charming garland too.

## FEATURED TECHNIQUES
Appliqué
Vest construction

## MATERIALS LIST

Child's vest pattern, size 2, 4, or 6
½ yd. fabric for bodice
½ yd. fabric for lining
⅛ yd. golden brown for gingerbread
⅛ yd. red & white stripe for candy canes
18" x 40" lightweight batting
3 – ¾" buttons
About 2 cupfuls stuffing (enough to stuff candy cane & one gingerbread man)
2 – 2" x 8" strips woven fusible interfacing
6 strands embroidery floss for gingerbread men (optional)
NOTE: seam allowances are ⅝", unless noted.

## INSTRUCTIONS

•Cut out bodice. Iron interfacing onto wrong side of fabric on both center front pieces. This will help stabilize the fabric for the buttons & buttonholes. Sew shoulder seams, joining fronts to the back sections. Lightly mark position for appliqué shapes and pocket. Cut out gingerbread. At this point, it's a good idea to embroider the faces, using 2 strands of 6-strand embroidery floss. Appliqué in position.

**Candy Canes**

•Cut bias strips 1½" x 6", fold in half, wrong sides together, sew using ¼" seams. Using Celtic press bars,

Alexandra Capadalis Dupré, Long Beach, NY, is a fiber artist who has been making quilts and wearable art since 1988. She has won numerous awards, including an Award of Excellence at the AQS/Hobbs Fashion Show. Alex enjoys teaching and lecturing, focusing her classes on innovative techniques from traditional patterns. She is currently working on a book to be published by AQS.

Alexandra Capadalis Dupré

iron, centering seam. Appliqué these in the shape of a candy cane, gathering the inside curve slightly. Be sure to turn in edges at each end as you appliqué. Appliqué the candy canes in place; the two that cover the side seams will be added after the side seams are stitched.

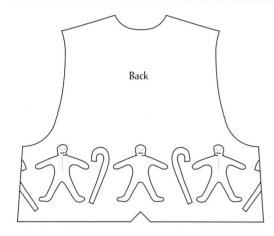

Back

### Pocket
•Cut out 2 pockets from pattern. Cut a bias strip from the candy cane stripe 1¼" x 4¼". Fold in half (wrong sides together) and align the raw edges with the top edge of the pocket (on the right side of fabric). Baste in place. Place two pockets, right sides together and sew, using a ⅝" seam allowance. Be sure to leave a small opening (approx. 1") at the bottom. Turn the pocket, slipstitch opening closed. You can then sew the pocket on by hand, or use your blind hem stitch on your machine.

•Cut out bodice in lining fabric: Cut out batting, loosely basting it to wrong sides of lining. Sew shoulder seams. Trim batting as close to seam as possible.

•Place lining and bodice, right sides together and pin in place. Notice that side seams are not sewn! Sew all the way around each arm hole. Start at the front lower edge and sew around the entire front edge of the vest

and neck. Sew along lower back edge. The side seams are all open. Trim all seams to ¼" and clip curves. Now you are ready to turn the vest. Take your time. Turn the vest by pulling it through one side seam. This can be tricky, but do it slowly so that you don't rip seams! Once you've turned it, give it a good pressing along the edge.

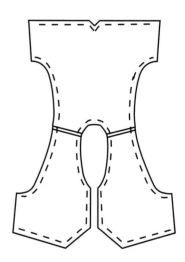

### Sewing the side seams
•Align the vest to match the front and back side seams. Working on one side at a time, match the right sides of the vest sides together, pin and stitch the side seam. Trim the seam allowance to ¼". Turn the lining fabric in and blind stitch in place. Repeat for other side seam. Appliqué the candy canes over the stitched side seams.

### Buttonholes
•One accurate way to make buttonholes on quilted garments is to trace the outline of the vest on to a nonwoven stabilizer such as Stitch 'n Tear. Do this for both sides of the vest. Then mark the exact size and location of each buttonhole and button. Baste the stabilizer to the vest and baste additional stabilizer to the back of the piece. This leaves no chance for error. Buttonholes can be difficult on quilted garments, especially on the

return side of the buttonhole. Since you've marked the exact length of the buttonhole, you can keep your machine stitching until it reaches your starting point. When it comes to sewing on buttons, tape the buttons onto the stabilizer to keep them from slipping. Then sew them on with your sewing machine. You can now rip off the stabilizer! You're ready to quilt. It's your choice, hand or machine or a little of both! Embellish the gingerbread men with beads, if you wish.

## Candy Cane

•Cut a bias strip, 1½" x 6". With right sides together, sew a ¼" seam. Stitch one end closed. Turn inside out. Stuff the candy cane with polyester fiberfil. Use a wooden chopstick to stuff the fiberfil. Sew the end

closed (at this point it will look like a stick). Bend one end until your are satisfied with the shape and sew it to hold in place.

## Gingerbread Man

•Cut out two gingerbread men, adding ¼" seam allowance to pattern. On one, embroider face and sew on beads. With right sides together sew, using a ¼" seam, leaving a small opening to turn. Once you've turned the gingerbread man, stuff it with polyester fiberfil. Use a wooden chopstick to push the fiberfil into the arms and legs. Slip stitch closed. Quilt the gingerbread man around the neck to give a little more definition. You could even stuff in a musical button.

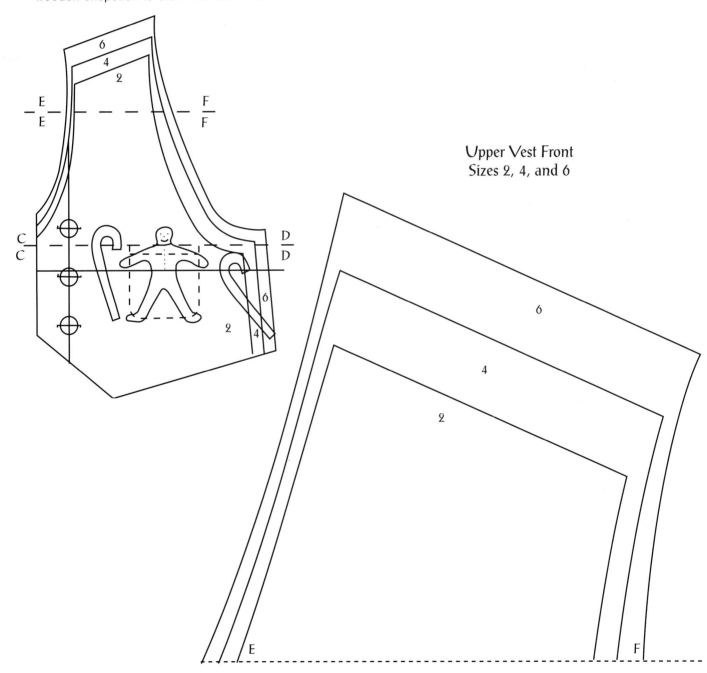

Upper Vest Front
Sizes 2, 4, and 6

## Upper Vest Back
### Sizes 2, 4, and 6

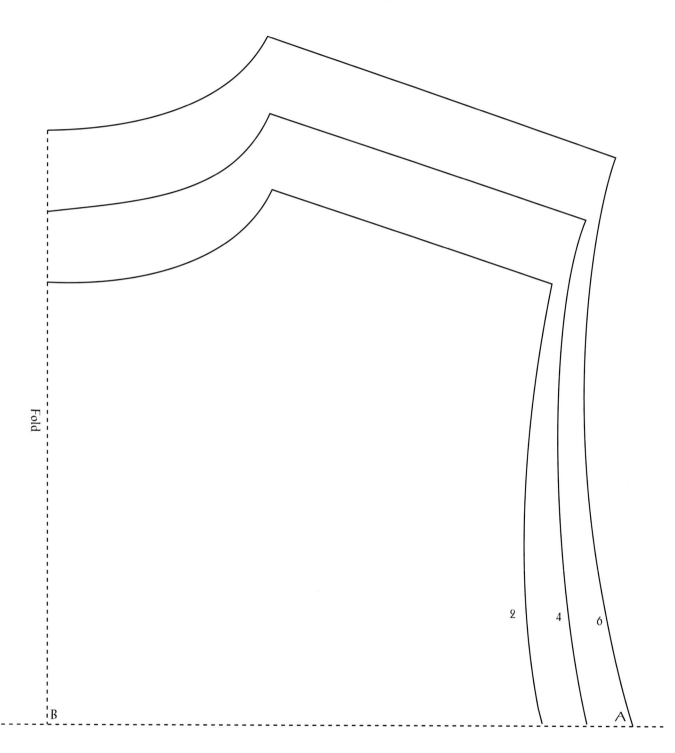

Fold

B

2    4    6

A

# CANDY CANE EXPRESS

Lower Vest Back
Sizes 2, 4, and 6

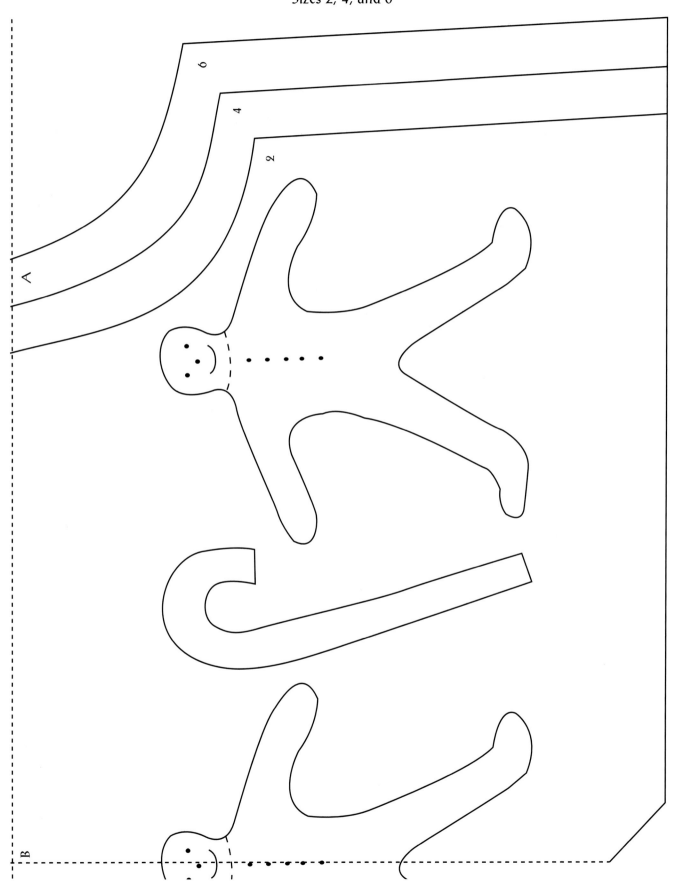

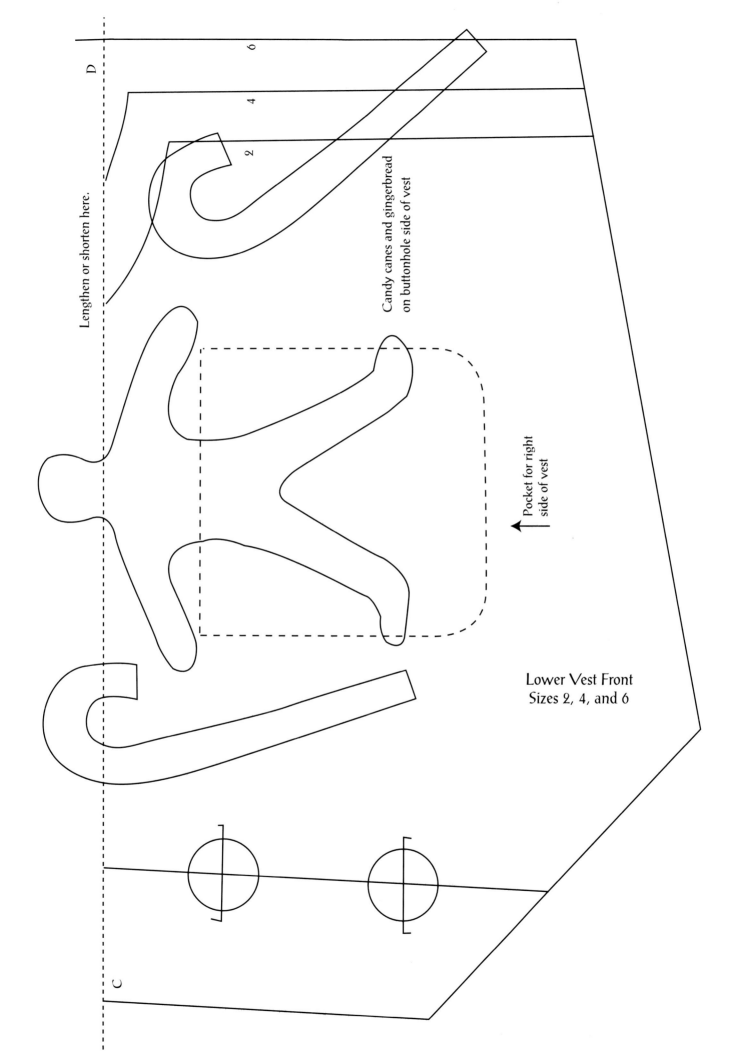

Lengthen or shorten here.

D

6

4

2

Candy canes and gingerbread
on buttonhole side of vest

Pocket for right
side of vest

Lower Vest Front
Sizes 2, 4, and 6

C

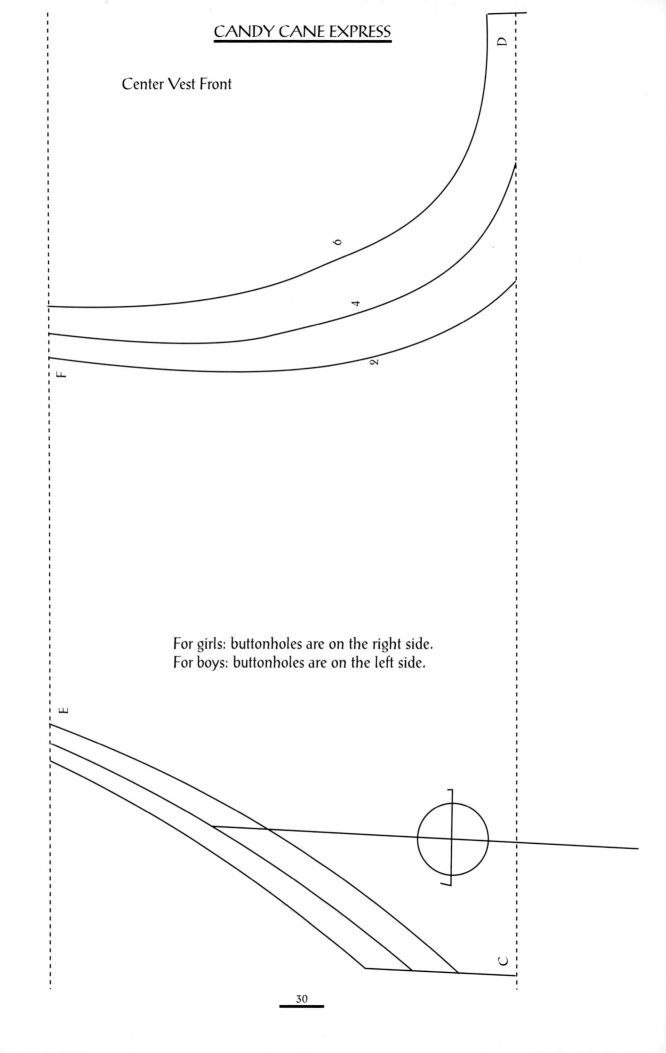

# CANDY CANE EXPRESS

Center Vest Front

For girls: buttonholes are on the right side.
For boys: buttonholes are on the left side.

30

# CHRISTMAS AND LOVE
## WALLHANGING

### by Kathy Fawcett

Machine piecing and machine quilting are combined with special marbled fabrics in Kathy Fawcett's 27½" x 19½" Christmas and Love wallhanging. It would be a perfect way to send your love to someone special at Christmas time.

## FEATURED TECHNIQUES
### Machine Piecing
### Machine Quilting

## MATERIALS LIST

1¼ yd. red cotton for blocks and backing
½ yd. green for binding and borders
Scraps of marbled or Christmas fabric for hearts
Batting
(Be sure to pre-wash fabrics.)

## CUTTING

•Cut 2 borders 1½" x 30"

•Cut 2 borders 1½" x 22" long

•Cut binding 2½" wide. Connect strips to have approximately 100" length for finishing. Press in half lengthwise.

•Cut backing from red approximately 30" x 24"

•Using templates (add ¼" seam allowance), cut 6 of template A and 6 of template B from marbled or Christmas fabric. (If you are using a fabric with a directional print, be very careful to follow the grain lines in the same direction on the fabric.)

•From the red fabric, cut:

    24 - C
    6 - D
    6 - E
    6 - F
    2 - G
    7 - H
    1 - 3½" x 18" strip

Kathy Fawcett's permanent address is Livingston, TX, but for the past ten years she and her husband have been traveling all across the U.S. in their motor home. She has been quilting for 15 years, teaches quiltmaking, and enjoys taking classes to learn more about quilting. Kathy co-authored with Carol Shoaf, **Marbling Fabrics for Quilts: A Guide for Learning and Teaching**, AQS.

Kathy Fawcett

## BLOCK ASSEMBLY

Referring to the diagram, attach as follows:

B + C + C
A + C + C
BCC + D
ACC + BCCD
Attach F to the side.
Attach E to other side.

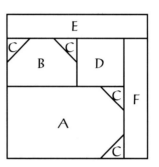

Add ¼" seam allowances.

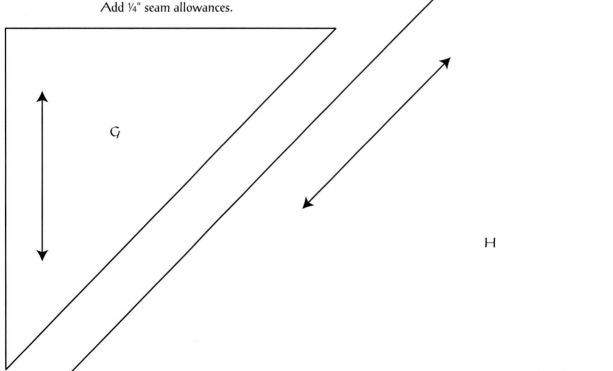

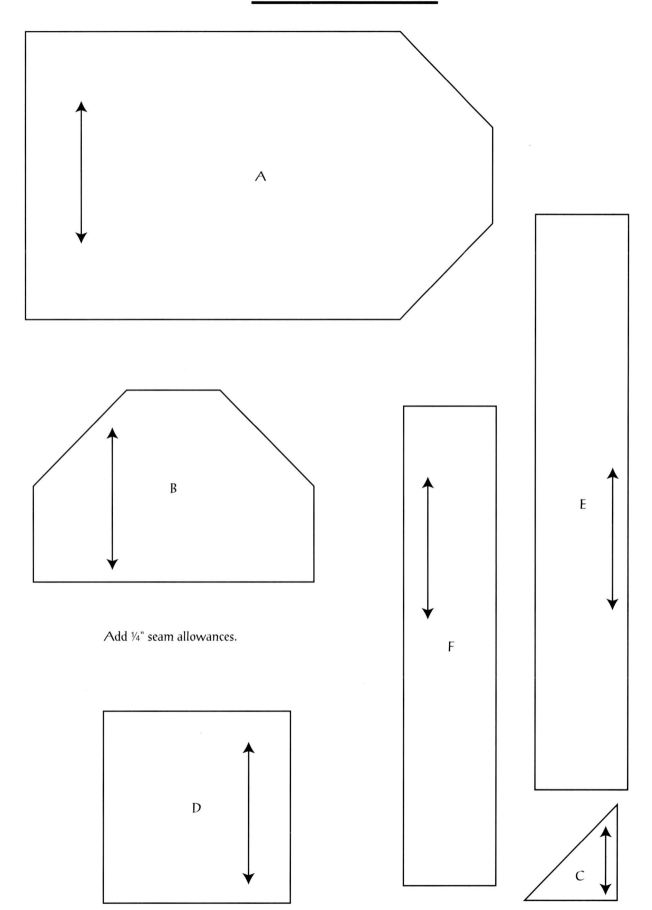

Add ¼" seam allowances.

## Assembly Diagram

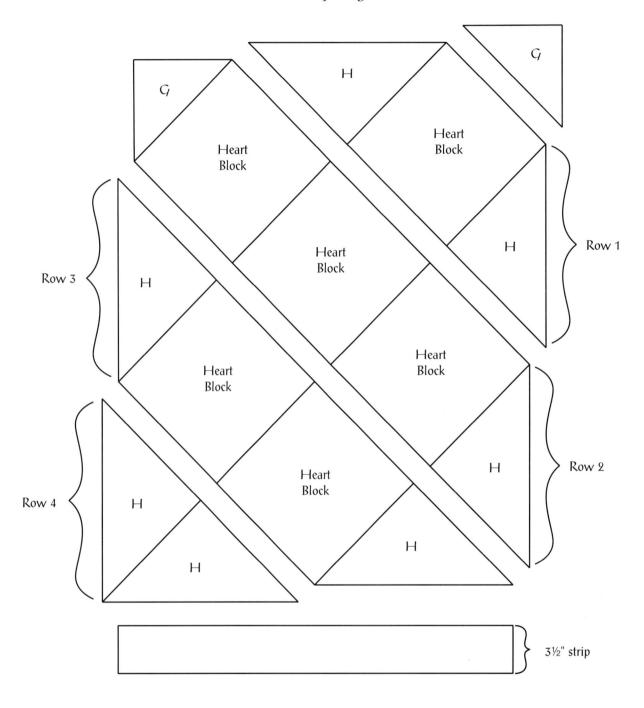

• Assemble in rows (1, 2, 3, 4). Add G and H triangles as shown in Assembly Diagram.

• Join rows as in diagram.

• Add "G" (upper right corner).

• Cut 3½" strip and add to bottom.

• Add borders.

• Quilt as you wish, and bind. This wallhanging is machine quilted in the ditch around each heart, and randomly machine tacked.

# CHRISTMAS BELT

### by Virginia Avery

Virginia Avery's Christmas belt is the perfect accessory for your holiday dress. And, you can select your own special beads, charms, and threads to embellish it.

## FEATURED TECHNIQUES
### Embellished wearables

## MATERIALS LIST

7" x 15" red satiny fabric
7" x 12" white satiny fabric
7" green square for tree
6" gold lamé square for stars and crescent
¼ yd. fabric for backing
Cotton batting
Fusible webbing, paper backed
Beads and charms for embellishment
2 skirt/pants hooks for closure

## INSTRUCTIONS

•Using belt pattern, cut one of lining and one of cotton batting. Use red and white fabric pieced as shown on belt; lay pieced fabric over batting and stitch through all layers with a machine decorative stitch, using metallic thread.

•Iron a fusible web to the wrong side of the green fabric for the tree. Trace tree outline on fusing material; cut. Remove protective paper and place tree in place on belt surface. Fuse following manufacturer's directions.

•Repeat fusing procedure on gold metallic fabric for stars; trace shapes, cut out, place on belt and fuse.

•Using metallic thread, stitch randomly (as shown on belt) over tree to anchor it securely. Using a straight stitch, stitch close to edge of stars and crescent moon.

•Decorate and embellish as you choose, using beads and/or charms.

Virginia Avery, Port Chester, NY, is a well-known garment designer and appliqué artist. Virginia travels around the world to teach her creative clothing, focusing on making original clothing through the creative use of fabrics, simple garment shapes constructed using even simpler sewing techniques. She is the author of **Wonderful Wearables**, AQS and other books on clothing and accessories.

Virginia Avery

•Cut *belt back* 6" wide and 21" long (or less, according to your measurements). Cut one layer batt 3" wide and 21" long.

•Line up batting along one lengthwise edge and pin in place, then stitch through batting and fabric ¼" from center of belt back band. Fold band in half lengthwise, right sides together. Stitch raw edges together, down the long side and across one end. Trim batt close to stitching, and trim seams at corner. Turn and press.

•Lay belt back on right side of belt front, matching raw edges of back to raw edges on end of right side (belt will fasten on left side of body). Place belt front lining over belt and belt back band, right sides together, and pin in place, centering back band over end of belt front. Starting at top edge of belt on left side, stitch ½" from top to end, pivot, stitch across end, catching the back band, then complete stitching along the bottom edge of belt front. Turn to right side by pulling on belt back, then press.

•Tuck in raw edges of left end of belt front and hand stitch; sew two skirt/pants hooks at end; be sure your stitches do not come through to the right side. Try belt on, mark with pin, and sew other half of hooks to belt band. Add your label. Wear with pleasure, listen to the compliments, and enjoy the looks of envy.

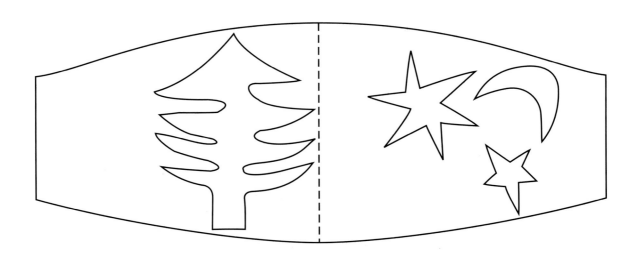

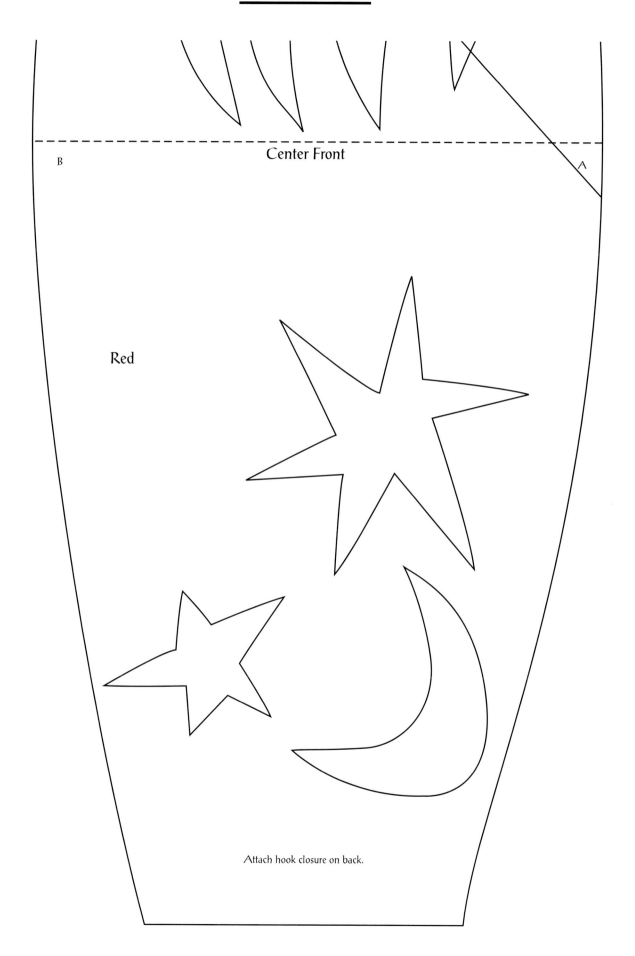

B

Center Front

A

Red

Attach hook closure on back.

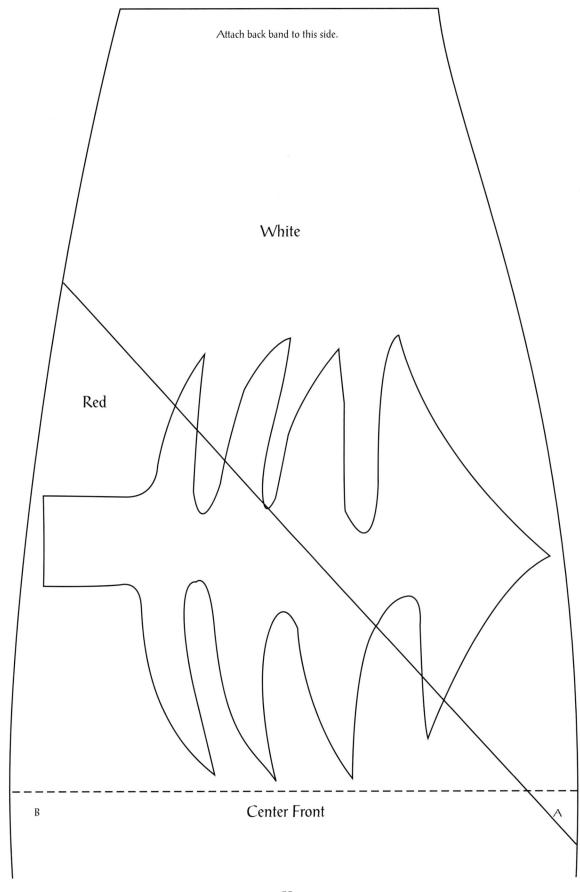

Attach back band to this side.

White

Red

B

Center Front

A

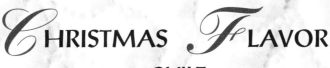

# CHRISTMAS FLAVOR

## QUILT

**by Jennifer Amor**

Here's a Christmas project for the whole family. Everyone can draw a Christmas picture and make a handprint (or a baby footprint) for the border. Use red and green flavors of powdered soft drink mix to dye the solid colored squares, then play with fabric crayons and paints for the pictures and borders. Give this 33" x 33" quilt to grandma, or make a new one every year to decorate your home. You could have a "quilt party" for your children and their friends during the holidays – or invite your relatives or neighbors to join the fun.

**FEATURED TECHNIQUES**
Fabric dyeing with powdered soft-drink mix
Fabric crayon pictures
Fabric painting

## MATERIALS LIST

⅛ yard non-permanent press unbleached muslin, washed several times in plain hot water and air dried (don't use detergent, bleach, or fabric softener).

¼ yard pre-washed white poly/cotton blend (65% polyester) or white 100% polyester satin (NOTE: fabric crayons are only permanent on synthetic fabrics).

¼ yard lattice strip fabric

¾ yard white cotton for borders

1 yard backing fabric

1 yard batting

¼ yard binding fabric

4 packages powdered soft drink mix, 2 red, 2 green

2 cups boiling water

2 tablespoons salt

8 sheets typing or copy paper

Crayola Fabric Crayons

Black extra-fine point permanent marking pen

Red and green fabric paint

2 wide sponge disposable paintbrushes

## INSTRUCTIONS

**Dyeing**

•Cut washed unbleached muslin into 12 – 3" squares.

•Place 2 packages red powdered soft drink mix in a

Jennifer Amor, Columbia, SC, teaches quilt classes nationwide, specializing in bargello, machine cutwork, and wearable art. Author of **Flavor Quilts for Kids to Make**, AQS, she also teaches children to make quilts through the NEA-supported Arts in Education Program in South Carolina schools. Her work has won over 70 ribbons and has been exhibited and published internationally.

Jennifer Amor

2-cup container and mix in 1 tablespoon of salt and 1 cup of boiling water. Repeat in another container with the green mix.

•Wet 12 squares of unbleached muslin in water and place 6 in the red dye mix, 6 in the green dye. Allow fabric to soak in dye up to 2 days to achieve maximum color, then remove, squeeze out excess liquid and smooth squares onto a plastic tray or cookie sheet covered with plastic wrap. Be careful to keep colors separate. When completely dry, rinse each color briefly in small bowl of clean cold water and dry again. Steam press.

### Pictures
•Cut 10 pieces of copy paper 2⅝" square, and 2 pieces 7¾" square.

•Draw 10 small and 2 large Christmas pictures in pencil. Use Christmas cards, wrapping paper, or coloring books for inspiration. NOTE: this is a reverse printing process – like looking in a mirror. Letters, numbers, musical notes etc. must be backwards. An easy way to do this is to write the letters etc. correctly in pencil, then turn the paper over, hold it against a sunny window, and trace the letters (which are now backwards). Color the traced side. When you transfer the image to fabric, the letters will be correct.

•Color the designs with fabric crayons. Press hard for intense colors, lightly for pale colors, and leave the paper blank for white. Combine crayons to create new colors. NOTE: there is no true red, since magenta is hot pink. (Mix orange with magenta to make red.) Remember that your pencil lines will not transfer – only the crayons will appear on the cloth. All pencil lines should be traced over with crayon. To keep the back of the paper crayon-free, use a clean sheet of paper under each piece that you color.

•Cut poly-cotton fabric into two 8" squares and ten 3⅛"

squares. Cut polyester satin into two 8¼" squares and ten 3¼" squares.

•Make an ironing pad on a hard surface with a stack of newspapers covered with a clean white paper.

•Before transferring pictures to cloth, experiment with fabric scraps to determine correct heat and time. Remember, polyester melts at high temperatures! Center each picture, crayon side down, on a square of fabric, leaving at least ¼" seam allowance all around. Cover with a clean sheet of white paper and iron with a hot, dry iron (medium hot for polyester satin). Use even pressure all over the surface and move the iron slowly. Don't move the picture. Continue pressing until the image is visible throught the back of the paper. Colors should be bright and clear.

•A black permanent marking pen may be used to outline images and add details. Test first on a fabric scrap to be sure the ink does not "bleed."

•Trim two large pictures to 7¾" square, and ten small designs to 3" square.

•For more detailed information on working with fabric crayons and other simple surface design techniques, see Chapters 5 and 6 in *Flavor Quilts for Kids to Make*.

### Assembly
•Use the best small dyed squares in the corners (you will have two extra of each color), and the picture squares forming a central cross to make the Nine-Patch blocks. Press and trim to 7¾" square.

•Cut three 1½" wide strips of lattice fabirc. From this, cut two pieces 18" long, three pieces 16" long, and two pieces 7¾" long.

•Join a Nine-Patch to a large picture block with a 7¾"

piece of lattice. Repeat for the bottom blocks reversing the placement of the Nine-Patch. Sew a 16" piece of lattice to the top and bottom of the top row, and to the bottom of the bottom row. Join the two rows, carefully matching the center lattice. Add the two 18" pieces of lattice to the left and right sides to complete the square.

## Borders
•Fold the wallhanging vertically and measure along the fold. Repeat for the horizontal measurement. Both should be 18". If they are not, make adjustments in the border measurements before cutting.

•Cut three 8" wide border strips from white cotton. Cut

facturer's directions. Names can be added to the handprints with a permanent pen. See *Flavor Quilts for Kids to Make* for more information on making blocks and borders.

•Iron the borders and cut to fit. Sew the two side borders on first, then the top and bottom borders. Press seams into the lattice.

## Finishing the quilt
•Layer the quilt with backing and batting. Quilt by hand or machine as desired.

•Cut and fold a 6" x 33" strip of backing fabric to make

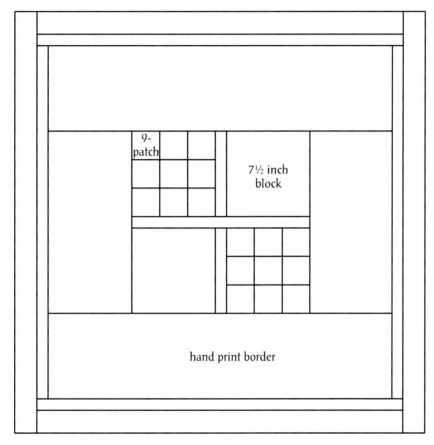

two of these 35" long, then mark an inch from each end for a 33" border. Cut two 20" pieces from the third strip, then mark an inch from each end for 18" borders.

•Experiment with the fabric paint on fabric scraps to get the right consistency for good handprints. Don't use too much paint. Keep it fairly dry, not runny. Paint that is too thick can usually be thinned with a little water.

•Set the borders, one at a time, on newspaper and make the handprints using fabric paint applied directly to the hands with a sponge brush. Use a dabbing motion, rather than a sweeping one which will leave streaks.

•When the paint is dry, heat set according to the manu-

a 3" sleeve for hanging the quilt. Pin the sleeve to the top raw edge.
•To bind with straight-grain binding, cut four 2" strips from the binding fabric. Fold each strip in half, lengthwise, wrong sides together, and press. Measure through the centers of the quilt for exact amounts. Cut 2 side binding pieces 33". Cut the top and bottom pieces 35" and turn in the raw ends to finish. Sew the binding to the back, matching raw edges. Pull the folded edge to the quilt front and top stitch close to the fold.

•Sew the sleeve bottom to the quilt back by hand or machine. Sign and date your work!

# CHRISTMAS FLORAL APPLIQUÉ
## WALLHANGING
### by Joyce Mori

As you look at this 24" x 24" floral appliqué project, you would probably never guess that the flower motifs were adapted from beadwork produced by various Native American Indian tribes. As quilters, we tend to look at the world around us as a source of inspiration for our designs, and often Native American designs are used in quilts. This wall quilt looks more Victorian than Native American! Study Native American arts and crafts as design sources for your quilts.

### FEATURED TECHNIQUES
Machine piecing
Applqué

## MATERIALS LIST

1 yd white/beige print
4" x 10" scrap white print
Fat quarter red Christmas print
Fat quarter dark green solid
¼ yd green Christmas print
Misc. scraps of Christmas colors plus purple, gold, dark blue, and green for flowers and leaves

•Does not include fabric for backing.

## INSTRUCTIONS

•Cut as follows:
**White/beige print**
    4 – B
    16 – E
    4 – G
    4 – D
    4 – Dr
    2 – 1 ½" x 22 ½" for border
    2 – 1½" x 24 ½" for border

**White print**
    4 – E

**Red Christmas print**
    16 – E
    8 – F
    4 – A

**Green Christmas print**
    4 – C

•Study the color photo to see how the quilt has been

The academic background in anthropology of Joyce Mori, Morgantown, WV, has provided her with knowledge of Native American design. The author of two AQS books, **Quilting Patterns from Native American Designs** and **Applique Patterns from Native American Beadwork Designs**, Joyce teaches and lectures on Native American designs for quilts and surface design ideas. The third book in this series will be soon be released by AQS.

Joyce Mori

sewn together.

•Cut four of Template B from the white/beige fabric. Add a ¼" seam allowance around the edge of this unit.

•Draw the floral appliqué design on the white/beige background fabric. Use your favorite brand marker or pencil.

•Make the stems by using ¼" bias bars. Appliqué the stems first. Then appliqué remaining floral and leaf motifs onto the background template B pieces.

•After you have finished the appliqué, sew a red template A on the top corner of template B. Sew a white template E onto the bottom corner of template B. Do this for each of the four white/beige template B pieces. You now have four squares. Sew these four blocks together. Appliqué a ¼" bias strip on the inside of the center square formed by white template E's. Appliqué the center flower (Appliqué 1) in place on the center square.

•Study the color photograph and line drawing of the quilt. Sew a corner unit by sewing a D and Dr to a C piece. Repeat this for the remaining three corners.

•Sew the pieced borders. Piece a white/beige template E to a red template E. Repeat this. Sew a red template F between these two bio-colored squares. Repeat this once more and sew a white/beige template G between these two strips. You have completed one border. Make three more of these borders. Sew borders onto the quilt, adding the four corner units.

•Add the final narrow white/beige borders.

## SUGGESTIONS

Quilt around the outside edges of the appliqué motifs. The background is filled in with parallel lines 1" apart. These lines are extended into the white/beige border units. The red corner units have parallel line quilting also. The narrow white/beige border is quilted with a meandering line.

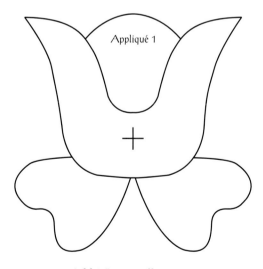

Add ¼" seam allowance.

Template B

Appliqué 2

1

2

3

Add ¼" seam allowances.

## Assembly Diagram

24" x 24"

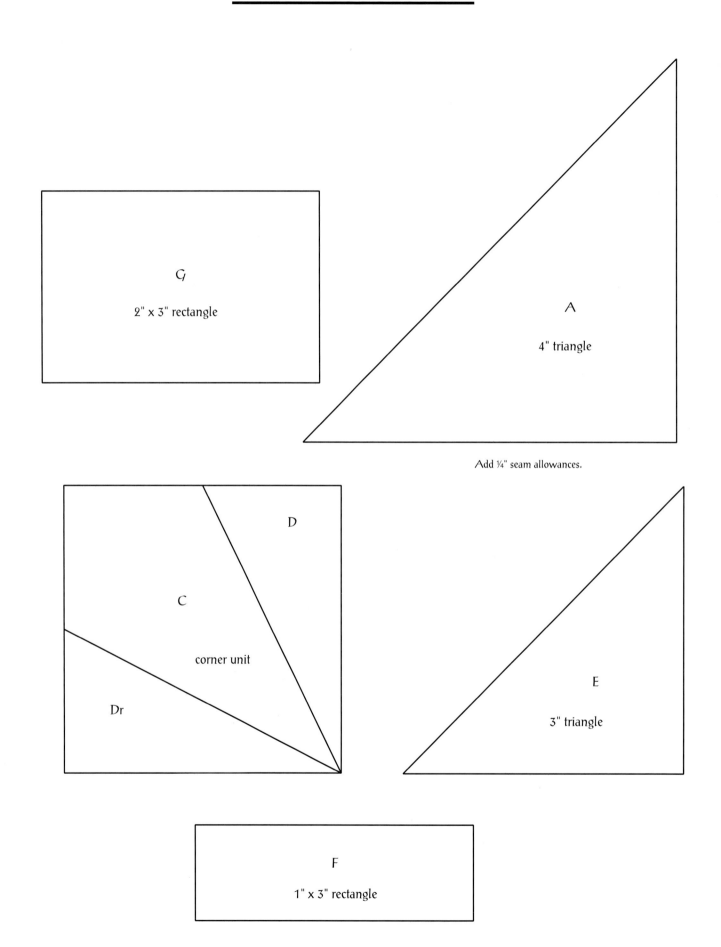

G

2" x 3" rectangle

A

4" triangle

Add ¼" seam allowances.

D

C

corner unit

Dr

E

3" triangle

F

1" x 3" rectangle

# CHRISTMAS PINEAPPLES
## WALLHANGING

**by Jane Hall**

Pineapples are a traditional sign of welcome. Jane Halls' Christmas Pineapples wallhanging will be the perfect welcome to your home during the holidays. Foundation piecing on paper makes the piecing precise and easy to do.

## FEATURED TECHNIQUES
## Foundation piecing

## MATERIALS LIST

For each block cut: 1½" center square
1" wide light strips, cut across the fabric for a total of 60"
1" wide dark strips, cut across the fabric for a total of 66"
12" x 2" strip for the corners
These fabrics can all be the same, or they can be a mixture of 2 – 6 different fabrics, some repeated.

## INSTRUCTIONS

•This nine-block wallhanging is constructed with 6" Pineapple Log Cabin blocks pieced on foundations for stability and precision. Lightweight paper or removable interfacing is the best choice of foundation material if you are piecing by machine. It is easy to remove and will not distort the stitch tension. If you are hand-piecing, use a lightweight fabric such as muslin for the foundations.

•Trace the block on tracing paper and replicate it by needle punching: place the traced design on top of a stack of 8-10 sheets of tracing paper. Pin in several places, and stitch along each line with an unthreaded sewing machine. After sewing the first few lines, the stack will be held in place by the punched holes. Each paper pattern will be identical to the others. If you are using muslin as a foundation, trace each block carefully, drawing all the lines, in one direction at a time.

•Dark value fabrics were placed on the diagonal planes

Jane Hall, Raleigh, NC, has been a quiltmaker for more than 20 years. She teaches, lectures, and judges quilts across the country. She likes to work with traditional patterns, using innovative colorations to create new graphics. Log Cabin designs are among her favorites. Jane and Dixie Haywood have co-authored two books; their third book, **Firm Foundations**, will be published by AQS in early 1996.

Jane Hall

and light value fabric on the horizontal and vertical planes. The same fabric was used for all the horizontal/vertical strips. The darkest fabrics were used in the corners of blocks on the outside edges of the quilt, creating an inner frame.

•Use *under* pressed-piecing: beginning at the middle of the block, pin the center square in place. The cut edges should overlap the drawn lines of the square, with ¼" seam allowance on all sides. Cut four pieces from the first strip of light fabric, each the size of one side of the center square. Lay the first piece of light fabric along one edge of the center square, right sides together, matching the cut edges. Pin, placing the pin at the lower edge of the strip.

•Turn the foundation over with the pinned fabric against the sewing machine feed dogs and stitch on the line, using a slightly smaller than usual stitch (12 – 14 per inch). It is not necessary to back-stitch, but begin and end two stitches at either end of the line. This is also necessary if you are sewing by hand. Trim the seam, if necessary, to a scant ¼", making sure any dark fabric will not shadow through. Open out the strip and pin it in place. It is important to keep this pin in place until the next row is sewn.

•To help keep the center squared, stitch the second strip to the opposite side of the square. Pin, turn the foundation over, stitch, trim, open, and pin as before. Attach the third and fourth strips. The block will look like a cross (Figure 1).

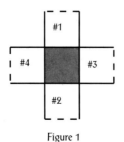

Figure 1

•The second row is pieced on the diagonal planes with dark strips. Using the drawn side of the foundation as a guide, cut four pieces of the first dark fabric the length of the line that will be sewn on plus an ample ¼" seam allowance at each end.

•To provide an accurate placement line for these strips, fold down the foundation along the sewing line and trim the excess fabric from the edge of the strips of the first row to a scant ¼" seam allowance. Take care not to cut too close to the folded foundation. When you fold the foundation back in place, you will have a fabric placement line for the strips for this second row. Lay them in place, sewing opposite sides as with Row 1, pinning, stitching, trimming if necessary, and pinning the strip open. You can pin the two opposite strips and sew them without removing the block from the machine, hopping from the end of the first to the beginning of the second. Remember to pin the strips open after stitching, leaving the pins in place. It is possible to make the entire block with four pins, moving them one at a time as the next strips are added.

•Continue to piece rows of four lights on the horizontal and vertical planes and four darks on the diagonals, until the corners are reached. After the third row of darks, you do not need to piece on opposite sides, and can lay up, pin, and stitch all four strips in one sewing, hopping from the end of one to the beginning of the next.

•The final diagonal strips form the corners, and will need a wider strip of fabric than cut for the other strips. It is possible to cut squares in half diagonally to make triangles for these corners, but if you use strips, the grainline will remain consistent in each plane.

•Press the block, and run a line of basting stitches a scant ¼" outside the outer line of the block. Trim foundation and fabric just outside that basting line. Do not remove the paper foundations at this time; they are the sewing lines for assembling the quilt.

•Join the blocks by matching the outer sewing lines. Stab pins at each corner and at each join along the sewing line. Bend back the seam allowance and check that the match is accurate. Move the pins if necessary; you should see a perfect chevron where the colors meet. Pin vertically and either stitch over the pins slowly or remove just as you come to them while stitching. Press these seams open, to retain the sharp points.

•Decide on borders to frame your quilt. Small inner borders with one of the bright colors in the blocks will enhance the overall look. Pineapple designs are best quilted to emphasize the graphic circles and wedges. These can be hand or machine quilted.

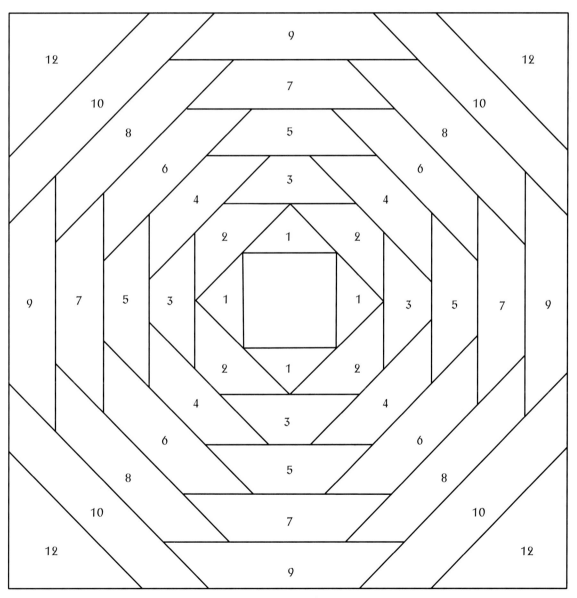

Pineapple

# CRAZY QUILT JACKET

## BERGDORF'S AGAIN

### by Janet Elwin

Sometimes our holiday wardrobe can come from unexpected places. Neighbor's, Polly & Ed McLaughlin, gave Janet Elwin some clothing items to recycle. Among them was a fabulous 50's black faille dress from Bergdorf Goodman's and a lovely very narrow silk tie from China. Aunt Edythe contributed a silvery fabric, and with lots of hints from Eila Tegethoff (who specializes in necktie crazy quilts), this wonderful crazy quilt jacket is sure to be a holiday favorite.

## FEATURED TECHNIQUES
## Crazy patch piecing with neckties

## MATERIALS LIST

2 yards muslin*
2 yards lining*
1 yard black faille
¼ yard silver decorated polyester
10 black silk ties, plain, patterned, and striped
Decorative threads; metallics, embroidery, anything glitzy
Approx. 10 yards of 1" black velvet ribbon
1 gorgeous button
Commercial jacket pattern

*These are the amounts of fabrics used for this favorite out-of-date Butterick pattern. Basically it is a vest with sleeves. Choose your favorite jacket pattern and alter the starred * fabric requirements.

## INSTRUCTIONS

•Set up iron and ironing board right next to your cutting area.

•Use pattern pieces for front of jacket, back, & sleeves.

•On muslin, lay out pattern pieces, leaving an extra 1" all around pieces, except jacket back. If jacket back is supposed to be cut on fold, follow those instructions. Many jackets have backs that are two pieces. If your pattern is like that, pin so you have 1" of muslin all around.

•Cut muslin 1" extra all around, except along fold where applicable.

Janet Elwin, Damariscotta, ME, has been exploring quiltmaking as a teacher, lecturer, and workshop leader since 1973. Her quilts have won more than 200 awards and have been exhibited across the U.S. and abroad. Starting with traditional designs and theories, she has used the hexagon and triangle shape to interpret her ideas into colorful, intriguing quilts and wallhangings. Janet is the author of **Ties–Ties–Ties** to be published by AQS in early 1996.

Janet B. Elwin

•Set iron on silk setting.

•Start with jacket back (you might get more creative as you go along and you want your best work in the front.) Cut a piece to fit in lower left corner of muslin. Cut your pieces of tie and faille pretty good sizes. The decorative part of the jacket will take up most of your time.

•Iron ½" seam under on all sides of pieces used for crazy piecing except outer garment edges. Pin in place.

•Cut another piece and iron under all edges ½". Lay to cover preceding piece. Lots of these pieces will overlap. If you can keep track, only iron under necessary edges. It is just as easy to iron under all edges, just in case placement is changed.

•Continue cutting shapes. Be creative. Cut some with a gentle curve, cut some with jagged edges. Iron under and pin on muslin.

•Fill up all spaces on jacket back and set aside.

•Work on sleeves next. Mark muslin right and left as some sleeves are noticeably different.

•When sleeves are covered with ties/faille, set aside.

•The most important part of the jacket is the front. Now that you have a little experience filling in spaces, arrange pieces to cover jacket fronts. Mark muslin front pieces left and right.

•At this point, you probably aren't too excited about the looks of the jacket. Trust me, the addition of all the embroidery will transform this "ugly" duckling into a swan.

•Fold velvet ribbon in half, lengthwise, and baste along edge. Measure around jacket edge, add a couple of inches and set aside this amount of velvet. Tuck rest of velvet under pinned-down edges of ties, here and there, adding a bit of texture.

•Machine edge stitch as close to edge as possible along all turned under edges using black or clear nylon thread.

•Now is where the fun begins but do not be in a rush. Machine embroidery takes time. Look at different sections on the jacket. Try to find an embroidery stitch and thread that will compliment that area. Do as little or as much in each section as pleases you. Some threads were too thick to run through the machine. These were laid along the edges and zigzagged in place using a matching thread.

•Iron all pieces putting fabric and embroidery face down on ironing board and iron on muslin side.

•Now you are ready to cut out the jacket pieces. Place all pattern pieces on proper crazy quilted muslins. Cut along pattern cutting lines.

•Follow all directions for jacket assembly. Before adding facings, baste velvet ribbon around edge of jacket using pattern ⅝" sewing line as guide. Ribbon should be basted using only ⅛" seam allowance.

•Lots of jackets today are unlined. If you want your jacket lined (evening jackets usually are lined) just cut jacket backs, fronts and sleeves from lining fabric using pattern pieces. Stitch jacket lining front and back together. Baste, wrong sides together, to crazy quilted jacket along edges. At this point add facings all around. Pin in sleeve lining and hem in place along sleeve armhole and edge.

•Add buttonholes and buttons.

# FOLK VILLAGE
## WALLHANGING

**by Lois Tornquist Smith**

This folk village wallhanging was inspired by a Christmas greeting received from friends in Belgium. A visit to a Belgium friend's home in December had earlier revealed a very simple but refreshing mode of holiday anticipation which centered more on the Christmas stories and family gatherings than the elaborate decorating and trimming so prevalent in some areas. This Folk Village depicts a town waiting silently and expectantly for Christmas without reference to the familiar decorations.

**FEATURED TECHNIQUES**
Machine piecing
Faced appliqué
Blind stitch appliqué

## MATERIALS LIST

¾ yd. blue sky fabric – dotted if possible
1 yd. white cotton sateen or other white cotton
Assorted solid scraps in primary colors
½ yd. lightweight white fabric for facing houses
½ yd. lace fabric that can be cut apart for snow shadows
½ yd. red for borders
¼ yd. green for binding
2 pks. red cording (optional)
1½ yds. backing fabric
Low loft or needle-punched fleece for batting

## INSTRUCTIONS

• Make a full scale master pattern on paper. (Two pieces of freezer paper taped together can make a 35" square.)

• Use templates given for basis of design or have design enlarged at a copy shop.

• Play with your village design; add your own shapes.

• Place another piece of freezer paper over master pattern.

Lois Tornquist Smith, Rockville, MD, is a certified teacher and judge. Her classes have inspired many to quilt using innovative techniques with the sewing machine. She is the author of **Fun and Fancy: MACHINE QUILTMAKING**, AQS. Her quilts have won awards at shows across the country; one of her quilts is in the permanent collection of the Museum of the American Quilter's Society, Paducah, KY.

Lois Tornquist Smith

•Trace off design.

•Label houses and rooftops with identifying letter or number.

•Cut out individual elements and iron to selected fabrics. (Shiny side of freezer paper will adhere to fabric.)

•Cut out elements adding accurate ¼" seam allowance to fabric as you cut.

## BACKGROUND

•Cut sky fabric 25" by 32" wide.

•Cut  snow fabric 10" by 32".

•Seam sky and snow sections together.

## PIECING

•Piece church steeple. Press under all raw edges except lower edge.

•Piece individual houses leaving outside edges raw, and press carefully.

•Join houses together into a long row. Outside edges of houses will still be raw. Press.

•Piece foreground house. Press.

•Optional extra snow: to achieve the rounded look of fresh snow on the roof tops, an extra piece of batting can be laid upon the under side of each roof.

•Using roof template, cut fleece or batting the size of roof without seam allowance.

•Position fleece on wrong side of roof top. Pin in place.

•Cut small pieces of lace and arrange on roof tops as desired.

•Using darning foot and white thread, follow designs of lace and stitch to roof.

## FACING

•Place row of houses right sides together upon lightweight white cotton.

•Stitch (¼" seam allowance) outside edges of design together sewing slight curves at bottom edge of houses to mimic mounds of snow.

•Slit facing fabric and turn houses right side out. Use a point turner to get sharp angles. Press carefully.

•Face foreground house.

## APPLIQUÉ

•Place steeple and houses on background.

•Press under the raw edges of trees and position as desired.

•Use a blind hem stitch to appliqué pieces to background.

•For hand appliqué use a small, tight stitch and thread to match appliqué.

•For machine appliqué, use clear invisible nylon thread and the blind hem stitch (not foot) on the machine. Use a small straight stitch and a zig zag stitch that just catches appliqué. Straight line of stitches should be so close to the appliqué that they do not show.

•If your machine does not have a blind stitch, stitch on the very edge of the appliqué with invisible nylon thread.

## THE QUILT SANDWICH

•Cut backing and batting the same size as pieced background.

•Layer and pin the three layers together.

•Quilt the house outlines by stitching in the seamline. Use invisible thread.

•More snow: Add lace and stitch in place using matching thread and free motion stitching.

•Add cross to steeple if desired.

•Quilt sky using clamshell pattern or a simple quilting design.

•To mark clamshell quilting design, cut two 2½" by 15" strips from freezer paper. Carefully fold papers into 2½" accordion style strips. Using compass set at 1¼" radius, draw top half of clamshell on folded paper strips. Cut on drawn line, cutting through all folded layers. Iron paper clamshell strip to sky fabric. Using darning foot and dropped feed dogs, gracefully stitch curved designs using freezer paper as guide. Reposition freezer paper and continue stitching.

•A simple free motion design can also be used to quilt sky.

•Square up wallhanging and edit with your rotary cutter.

•Add borders as desired. Pictured borders include: cording, border (1" finished white and 2" finished red), green binding (cut 2" and folded in half.)

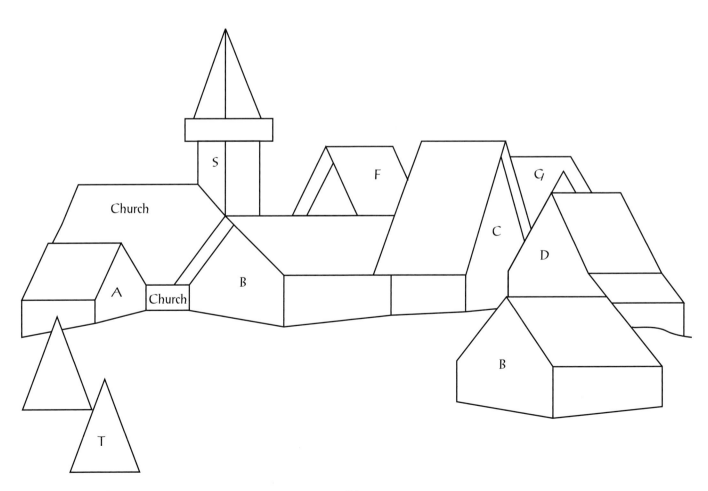

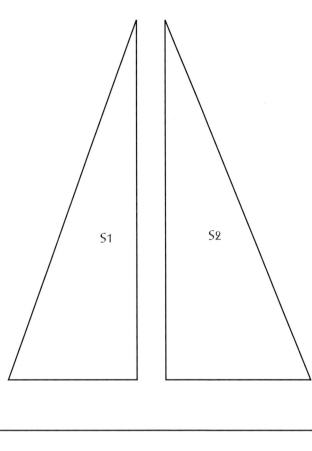

S1

S2

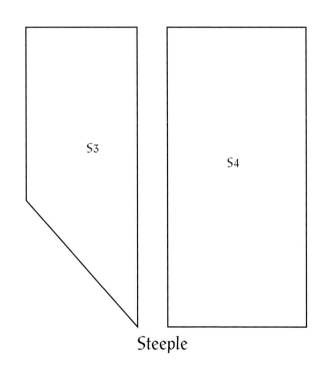

S3

S4

Steeple

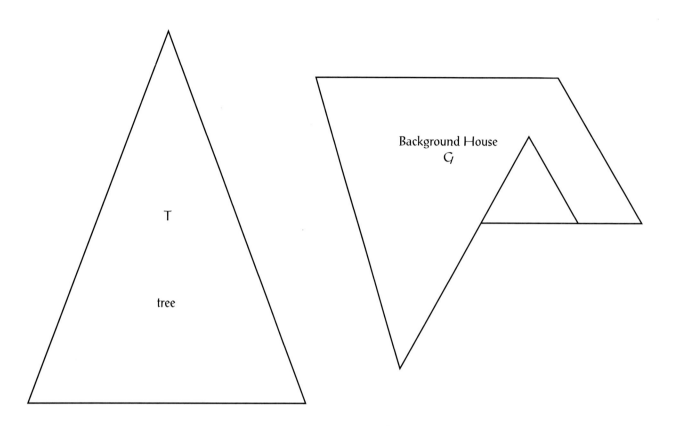

T

tree

Background House
G

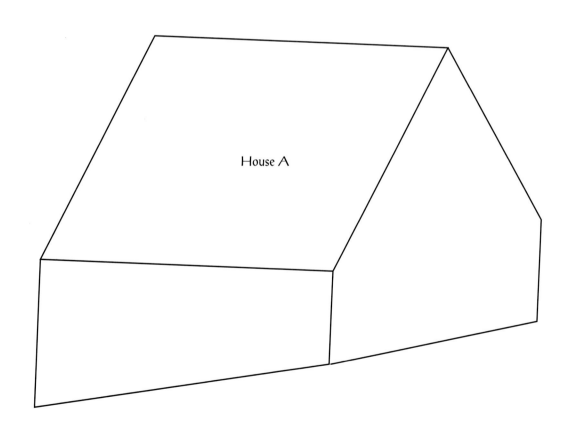

House A

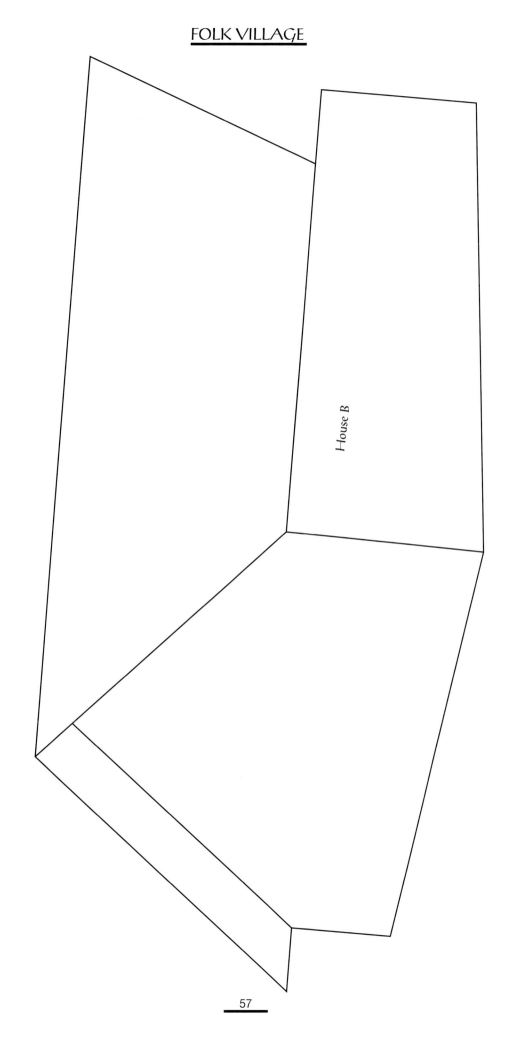

House B

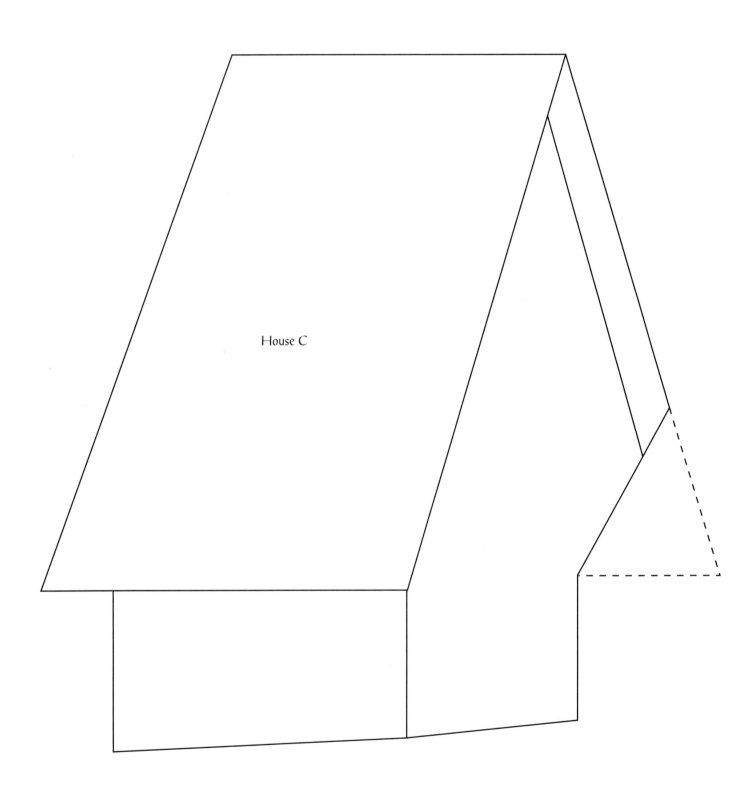

House C

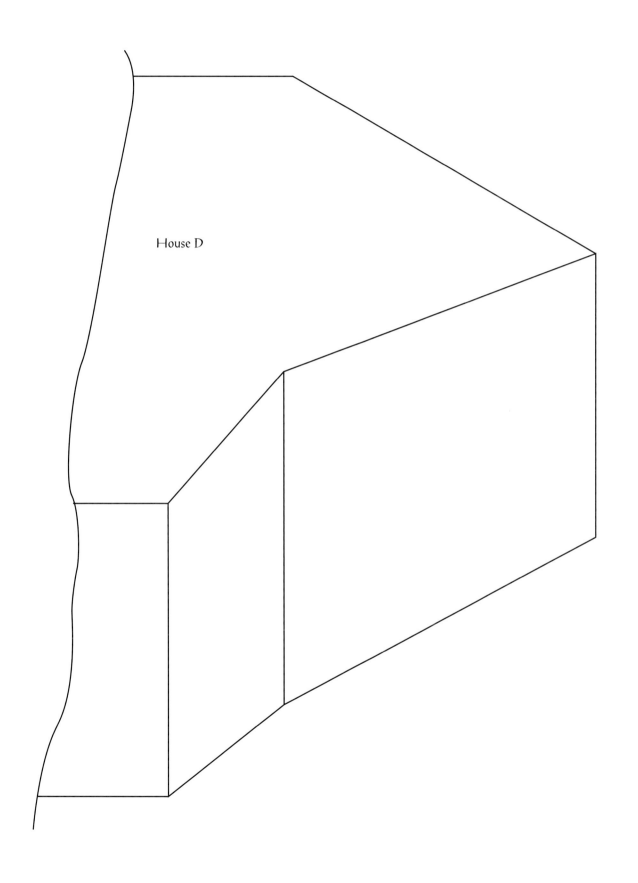

House D

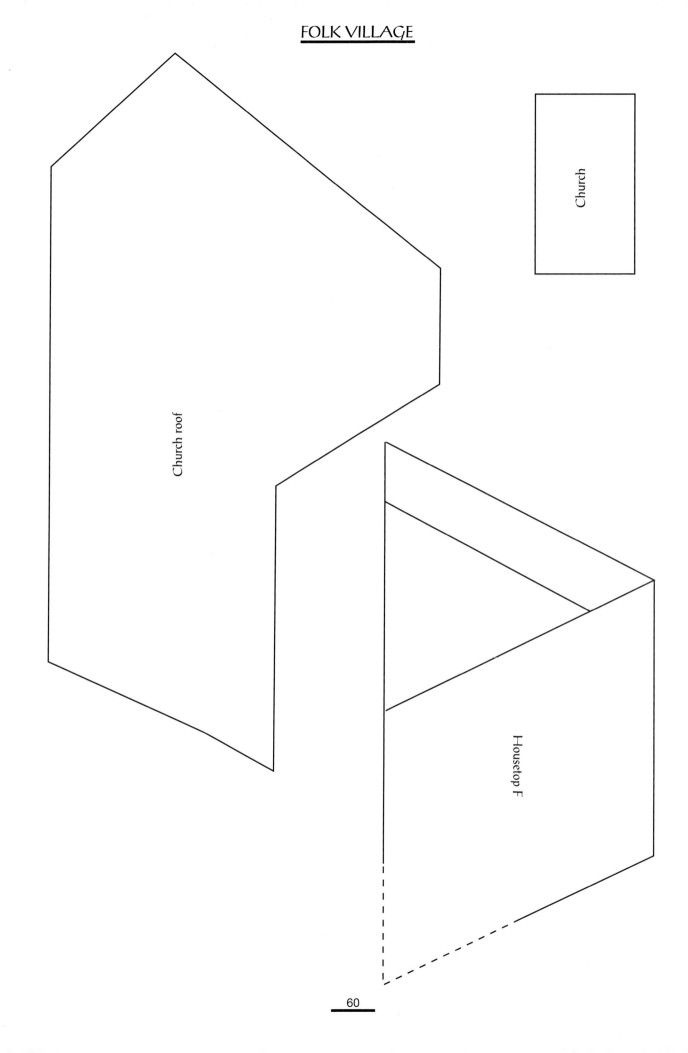

Church

Church roof

Housetop F

# ℋexagon ℘atchwork
## CHRISTMAS STOCKING

by Tina M. Gravatt

English piecing of hexagon shapes are combined with a variety of plaid fabrics to make this 11½" X 16" candy cane looking stocking. It's easy to do by hand – a fun project to carry with you to complete.

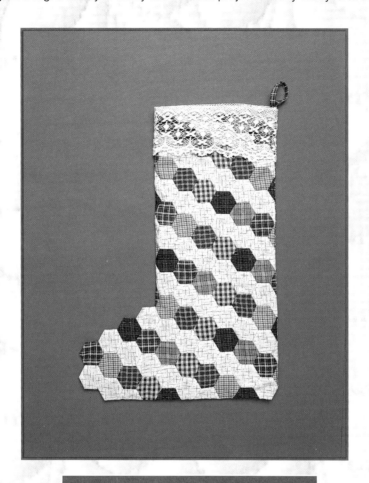

### FEATURED TECHNIQUES
### English hand piecing

## MATERIALS LIST

¼ yd. light print – A
⅛ yd. dark red and green plaid – B
⅛ yd. dark green plaid – C
⅛ yd. medium red and green plaid – D
⅛ yd. light red and green check – E
⅛ yd. dark red and green check – F
⅛ yd. medium red and green check – G
⅜ yd. backing and optional lining – H
½ yd. of crocheted edging or lace 3" to 4" wide
11" x 5" strip of one of the plaids or checks for loop to hang stocking.

**Cut Papers & Fabrics:**

•Light fabrics for light stripes
42 full hexagons
4 half hexagons
10 triangle section hexagons
1 corner section hexagon

•Red and green plaids and checks
42 full hexagons
3 half hexagons
10 triangle section hexagons
1 corner section hexagon

Tina M. Gravatt, Philadelphia, PA, started quiltmaking in the early 70's. Her interest in historically accurate miniature quilts began in 1985. Tina is well known as a teacher, lecturer, and author. She specializes in American and European historically accurate miniature quilts. Her work has been featured in magazine articles, and in her books, **Heirloom Miniatures** and **Old Favorites in Miniature**, AQS.

Tina M. Gravatt

•After hexagons are pieced, cut out backing adding ½" seam allowance (this is easier to handle and can be trimmed later) and 3½" longer at top. Cut out lining using pieced hexagons as pattern, adding ½" seam allowance (this must be trimmed to ¼" after being sewn in place).

## INSTRUCTIONS

•Cut papers from index cards. Inexpensive and rather flimsy cards are the best. Wrap the fabric over the

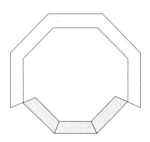

Figure 1

papers (see Figure 1) and baste through all layers. Use a light color quilting thread for basting (it is thicker and easier to remove later). With right sides together, whip-stitch seams together using matching color(s) all purpose sewing thread (see Figure 2). Try not to stitch through the papers. Assemble hexagons and partial hexagons according to assembly diagram, Figure 3. To create a candy cane effect, alternate rows of red and greens with rows of light color print. Stitch rows togeth-

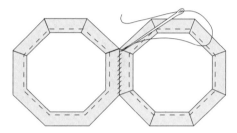

Figure 2

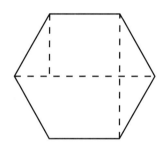

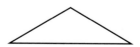

Templates

er to create stocking.

•Remove papers by clipping basting threads and pulling out papers. If you have caught the edge of some of the papers when you assembled the hexagons, don't worry, they will still remove easily. *Leave the papers in the outside edge row of full and partial hexagons*. These will stabilize the edges while you finish constructing the stocking.

•If the stocking is intended for other than decorative use, a lining should be added behind the hexagons to strengthen the stocking. This can be achieved by whip-stitching the lining to the outer edges of hexagons. As you begin to attach the lining to each patchwork piece, carefully remove papers trying not to distort the shapes.

•Finishing: Turn under ½" on top of stocking lining and press. Repeat and stitch hem in place through backing.

(Hem is to be on the inside of stocking.) Pin the backing to the front, trimming and clipping seams where necessary, and tucking them to the inside of the stocking. Sew front to back in the same way the hexagons were assembled. Papers may be left in until the backing is attached, or removed after a hexagon has been sewn to the backing. If they are removed before adding the backing, the shapes may distort. If the facing on the backing of the stocking did not get caught in the seam, hand tack in place.

•Add edging by hand sewing onto top of the stocking. It looks best if sewn on the inside and the edging folds out over the top to the front of the stocking.

•Fold in ¼" from both outside edges of the 1" x 5" strip. Press, fold in half and stitch closed. Hand sew a narrow strip onto the stocking and into the seam allowance for a hanging loop.

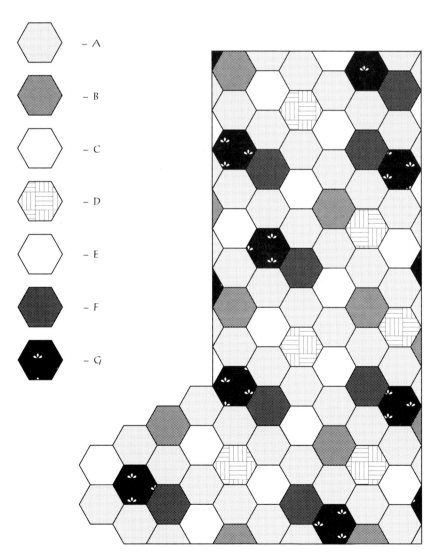

- A
- B
- C
- D
- E
- F
- G

Figure 3

# HOLIDAY GREETING CARDS

### by Carol Shoaf

Send your own holiday greetings by following Carol Shoaf's easy directions for making greeting cards. Purchased card stock, fabrics, and fusible web are the main ingredients for this quick and easy project.

## FEATURED TECHNIQUES
Fusible appliqué
Pen and ink embellishment

## MATERIALS LIST

One sheet 8½" x 11" card stock with matching A-2 envelope is required for each card; you can purchase at your local print shop.
⅛ yd. fusible web

**Poinsettia Card**
4" x 5" rectangle large peacock marbled fabric in light hunter green and burgundy for background oval
9" square mottled red to burgundy fabric for poinsettia
Gold Pen Touch pen
Red Pigma pen

**Jingle Bells Card**
4" x 5" rectangle small peacock marbled fabric in Christmas green and red with yellow highlights for background oval.
3" square of 2 different shades of green for leaves.
3" square of 3 different reds for bow.
9" square of golden yellow fabric for bells. Look for fabrics that give contour, for the curves of the bells.
4" square lighter yellow fabric for the bell's ridge.
3" square brownish fabric for the holes on the bell.
Pigma pens in black, brown, and red.

Carol Shoaf, Portland, WA, has quilted for over 20 years and is primarily interested in hand appliqué. To add realism to her work, she explored various techniques while creating her own fabrics. Carol and Kathy Fawcett co-authored **Marbling Fabric for Quilts, A Guide for Learning and Teaching**, AQS, to provide quilters with a good basic instruction manual on marbling fabrics.

Carol Shoaf

## INSTRUCTIONS

•Cut card stock to 5½" x 8½". Place 5½" edges together. Fold. Set aside.

•With black Pigma pen trace individual templates onto fusible web. Cut out leaving ⅛" around all edges. Repeat for background ovals.

•Iron fusible web onto the wrong side of fabric. Cut out templates on the line. Set aside.

•With pencil lightly trace design onto background oval. Leave paper backing on oval until entire design is ironed in place.

•Pull paper backing off template piece #1 as you iron design onto background oval following the number sequence.

•Pull paper backing off of background oval. Iron in place on card stock.

•For Poinsettia Card: Pen in center dots with gold Pen Touch pen. Outline gold with red Pigma pen.

•For Jingle Bells Card: Pen in stem with black Pigma pen. Draw in berries with red Pigma pen. In the ditch outline bell ridges with brown Pigma pen.

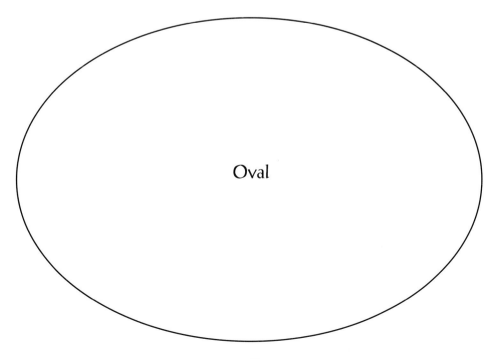

Oval

## Poinsettia

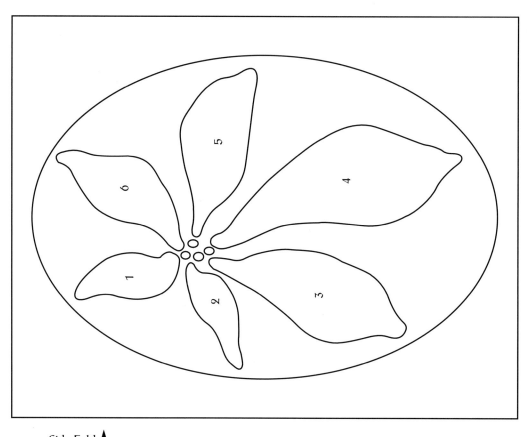

Side Fold ↑

## Jingle Bells

Top fold ↓

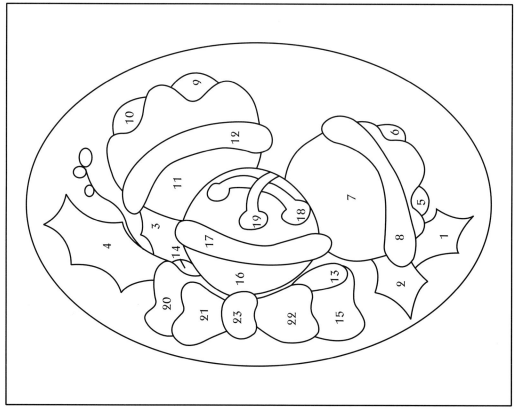

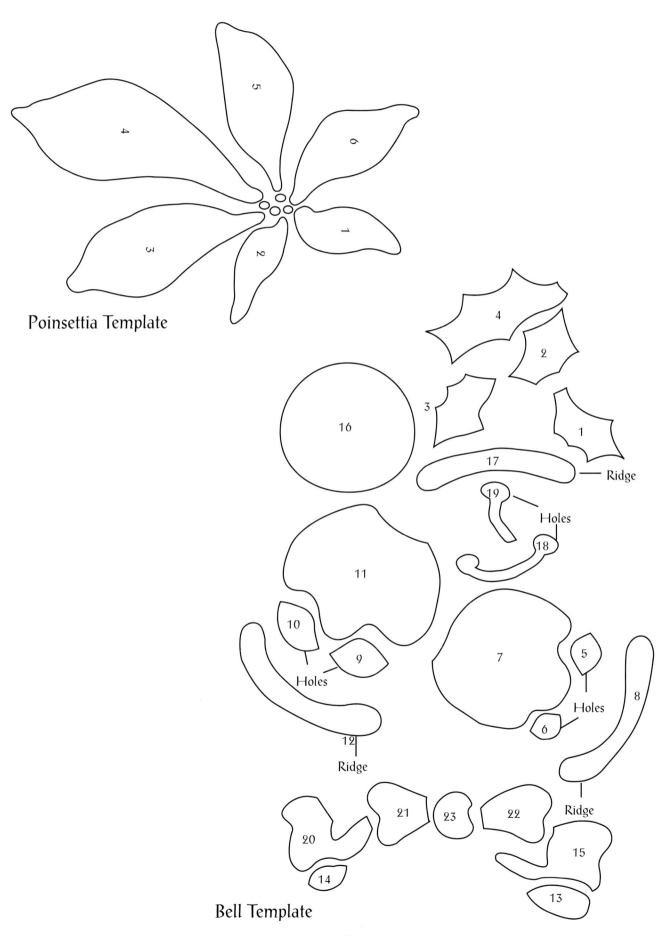

Poinsettia Template

Bell Template

# HOLIDAY LIGHTS

## WALLHANGING

**by Darra Duffy Williamson**

In "Holiday Lights" you will find the most unlikely red and green fabrics in the scrappy star and fan blocks. The undulating vine appliquéd border puts the finishing touch on this charming 29" x 29" wallhanging.

## FEATURED TECHNIQUES
### Machine piecing
### Appliquéd borders
### Bias strip vines

## SELECTING FABRIC

•When choosing fabrics for this – or any other – scrap quilt, be as liberal as possible in your interpretation of the color scheme. Not every fabric needs to match. When choosing the red and green fabrics for this quilt, consider the entire "family" of each color. Red can include everything from fire engine to pink, brick to burgundy, rust to rose. Green can range from forest to bright, Christmas to seafoam, teal to lime. If you study the photo of "Holiday Lights" carefully, you'll find the most unlikely reds and greens co-existing side-by-side! A liberal mix of neutrals such as brown, beige, and ecru help to pull it all together. And don't be afraid of a few

"zingers": a touch of super-bright red, look-at-me-green and/or mustard (yellow) brown will give this color scheme a special sparkle.

•When you are satisfied that you have chosen a wide and exciting range of pure hues, tints, and shades within your color scheme, check that you have also included a good selection of lights, mediums, and darks. Contrast in value adds depth and dimension to the design.

•Finally, assess your fabrics to be certain you have assembled a good mix of visual textures: florals and vines, dots and geometrics, abstract and picture prints

Darra Duffy Williamson, Blowing Rock, NC, is the author of **Sensational Scrap Quilts**, AQS, and numerous magazine articles. In 1989, she was named Quilt Teacher of the Year and has traveled extensively teaching at guilds and quilt events. Although Darra no longer teaches, she remains active quilting, designing, exhibiting, judging, collecting, and writing about quilts. She is currently working on her second book to be published by AQS.

Darra Duffy Williamson

both large and small in scale. Variety creates the visual richness that makes a scrap quilt such fun to explore!

## MATERIALS LIST

•100% prewashed cotton is recommended for use in this quilt. Yardage is estimated based on fabric that is 44/45" wide before washing.

•A wide variety of red, green, gold, beige, and ecru scraps for Star and Fan blocks, and leaf appliqués

•A "fat quarter" (18" x 22") of dark green print for the appliqué vines

•A "fat quarter" (18" x 22") of dark red subtle print for the inner border

•½ yard large scale light red floral for the setting triangles and outer border

•¼ yard dark red print for binding

•1 yard fabric of choice for the backing and hanging sleeve

•Batting approximately 33" x 33"

## CUTTING

•Full-size pattern pieces are included for the Star and Fan blocks, as well as for the setting triangles (E and F). Be sure to add ¼" seam allowances.

•For those who prefer "no template" techniques, alternative instructions are given for cutting the Star blocks and setting triangles with a rotary cutter.

•A full-size pattern piece is also included for the leaf appliqué. As is customary for hand appliqué, this pattern piece is the finished size and does not include a

seam allowance. Remember to add a scant ¼" seam allowance when cutting the leaves from fabric.

•Instructions for the vines and border strips are for quick-cutting with a rotary cutter. These pieces include ¼" seam allowances and are cut slightly longer than necessary to allow for adjustment. Trim them to the required lengths when they are added to the quilt.

•Cut pieces in the order shown.

•From the large scale light red floral, cut:
    2 strips: 5" x 44" for the outer borders. Divide
    each strip in half to make a total of four 5" x 22"
    border strips.
    4 – E triangles
    4 – F triangles
    Or
    1 square 9¾"; divide the square on the diagonal
    in both directions to make four E triangles.
    2 squares: 6⅞"; divide each square in half on
    the diagonal to make two F triangles.

•From the dark red subtle print, cut:
    4 strips – 2" x 22" for the inner borders
    4 – H pieces for the Fan handles

•From the dark green print, cut:
    1 square – 18" x 18" for the applique vines.
    Fold the square diagonally to find the true
    bias, trim off the fold, then cut:
    4 strips – ⅞" wide x the true bias. Since you
    are cutting double thickness, you will have a
    total of eight bias strips to use for the vines.

•From the assorted red, green, gold, beige, and ecru scraps of all values, cut:
    52 – leaf appliqués

•From the lighter value red, green, gold, beige, and ecru scraps, cut:

20 – B triangles
20 – D squares
Or
5 – 4¼" squares; divide each square on the diagonal in both directions to make 4 B triangles.
20 – 2" D squares

•From the medium and darker value red, green, and gold scraps, cut:
24 – G pieces for the Fan blades
40 – A triangles for the Star blocks
5 – C squares for the Star blocks
Or
20 – 2⅜" squares; divide each square in half on the diagonal to make two A triangles.
5 – 3½" C squares

•From the dark red print, cut:
3 strips – 2" x 44" on the crosswise grain for binding

# PIECING

### Star Blocks (6" finished)

•Refer to the Star Block Diagram and lay out the five Star blocks before you begin piecing them. A piece of white felt, flannel, or cotton batting makes a wonderful "design wall" for previewing the blocks before they are sewn. The shapes will cling to the nap of the "wall" without pinning, and you'll be able to arrange and rearrange the pieces to try any number of fabric combinations.

•Keep in mind that each fabric does not need to match every other fabric in the block. Mix and match the reds with the greens, the golds with the reds. In a scrap quilt,

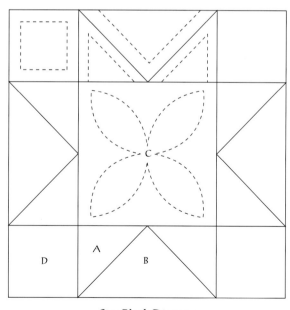

Star Block Diagram

it is the overall look that counts. In the quilt shown, red star points alternate with green in each block. You may prefer to make each star point in a block the same color. Or, for a totally random look, you can toss all of the A triangles in a brown paper bag and use them as they are drawn, grab bag style. Whatever method you choose, relax and have fun with the fabrics!!

### Sewing Star Blocks

•When you are satisfied with the arrangement of fabrics in the five Star blocks, you are ready to sew.

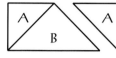

Figure 1

• Sew an A triangle to each side of a B triangle as shown in Figure 1. Press the seam allowances away from the B triangle. Make 20 of these A/B units.

• Sew an A/B unit to the top and bottom edge of a C square as shown in Figure 2. The seams in each A/B

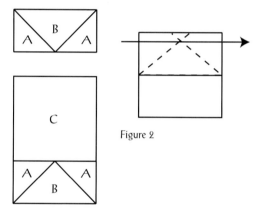

Figure 2

unit form an "X." Stitch through the "X" for a perfect point where the AB unit and the C square join. Press the seam allowances toward the C square. Make five of these units.

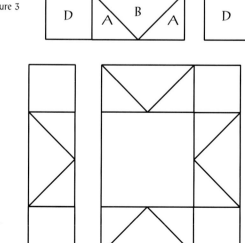

Figure 3

•Sew a D square to each end of the remaining A/B units as shown in Figure 3. Press the seam allowances toward the D squares. Make 10 of these units.

•Sew an A/B/D unit to the left and the right edge of each A/B/C unit as shown, pinning carefully to match the seams. Press as desired.

**Piecing the Fan Blocks**
•There are two options for adding the handle (piece H) to each Fan block. If you are comfortable piecing curves, the handle can be pieced into the block. A simple alternative is to appliqué the handle to the pieced fan blades. (That's the method I used!)

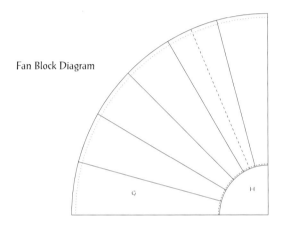

Fan Block Diagram

•Once again, use your design wall and lay out the four Fan blocks to find a pleasing balance of colors and values. When you are satisfied with the arrangement of the fabrics, you are ready to sew.

•Sew two adjacent G blades to form a pair as shown in Figure 4. If you plan to appliqué the fan handle (H) you can sew from raw edge to raw edge as usual. If you intend to piece the handle into the block, begin sewing ¼" from the raw edge on the narrow end of the blades and stitch to the raw edge as usual on the wide end.

• Join three pairs of fan blades to make a fan as shown. You'll have a total of four fans of six blades each. Press the seam allowances to one side.

•Piece or appliqué the fan handle to the pieced fan as shown in the Fan Block Diagram. if you choose to appliqué, turn the seam allowance under on the curved edge only. The straight edge will form the outer seam allowance for the block.

•Use your sewing machine to stay stitch along the outer curve of each Fan block as indicated by the dotted line in the Fan Block Diagram. Since the edge is

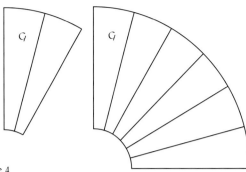

Figure 4

curved – and therefore bias – the stitching will prevent the block from stretching during subsequent handling.

**Assembling the Quilt Top**
•Refer to the Assembly Diagram and lay out the five Star blocks and the E and F setting triangles. The diagonal rows are numbered for easy reference.

•Sew the appropriate Star blocks, E and F triangles into diagonal rows, pressing the seam allowances in opposite directions from row to row.

•Join the rows, pinning carefully to match the seams. Press the seam allowances as desired.

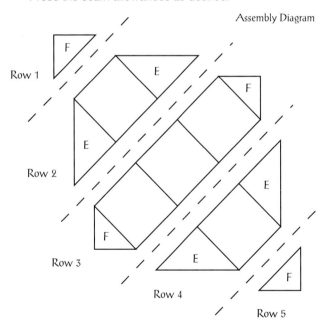

Assembly Diagram

•Sew a 2" x 22" dark red print inner border strip to a 5" x 22" light red floral outer border strip to form a single border unit as shown in the Border Diagram. Press the seam allowances toward the wider strip. Make four of these border units.

•Measure the quilt top through its vertical and horizontal center and trim the border units to this length. Crease each border unit to find its midpoint. Pin, then sew a border unit to the top and the bottom edges of the quilt. Match quilt and border at midpoints and ends first, easing as necessary to accommodate any fullness. Be certain that the dark red inner border is closest to the center of the quilt before you begin to sew! Press the seam allowances toward the border units.

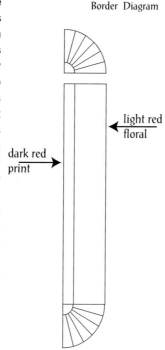

Border Diagram

dark red print →

← light red floral

•Sew a Fan block to each end of the remaining two border units as shown in the Border Diagram, carefully aligning the dark red inner border with the fan handles (H). Press the seam allowances away from the Fan blocks.

•Sew a border unit to the left and the right edges of the quilt top, pinning carefully to match the seams. Press as desired.

## Completing the Appliqué Borders
•Use your preferred method to prepare the leaves for appliqué.

•To make the vines, fold each of the dark green print bias strips wrong sides together, matching the raw edges. Stitch a scant ⅛" seam along the length of each strip (Figure 5). Using a touch of spray starch for crispness, press each strip. Center the seam to face you as you press. Bias press bars, made of heat resistant nylon, can be helpful with this step.

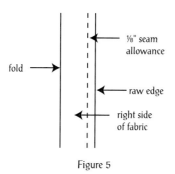

fold →

⅛" seam allowance

← raw edge

← right side of fabric

Figure 5

Refer to the Appliqué Diagram and quilt photo. Position, then pin or baste two vines and 13 leaves to each of the four borders, overlapping into the E triangles as shown. The vines should be positioned seam side down and trimmed as necessary. Use your preferred method of appliqué and thread to match the color of the appliqué to stitch the vines and leaves to the quilt. Tuck the ends of the vines under, and stitch the inner curves first to minimize stretching.

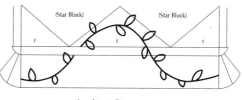

(Star Block)   (Star Block)

F       E       F

Appliqué Diagram

## Quilting and Finishing
•Use your preferred method to mark the quilt top for quilting. The dashed lines in the Star and Fan Block diagrams indicate how the blocks in this quilt were quilted. In addition, a small fan was quilted in each F triangle and in the center of each outer border. The appliqué was outline quilted, and the background of each E triangle and outer border was finished with ¾" cross-hatching for additional texture.

•Layer the backing, batting and quilt top; baste. Backing should extend approximately 3" on all sides. Trim the excess and set it aside to construct a hanging sleeve for the finished quilt.

•Quilt all marked designs. The quilt shown was hand quilted in red quilting thread.

•Use the 2" x 44" dark red strips to make double-fold binding. Because the strips are cut on the crosswise grain, they will have enough give to turn the gentle curves on the quilt's outer edges. If you prefer – and if you have sufficient fabric – you can make and substitute double-fold continuous bias binding. Apply the binding as described earlier. You will not need to miter the corners; simply ease the binding around the corner curves and pin generously before stitching.

•Finish the quilt with a permanent label that shows your name, date, and other pertinent information. Make a sleeve from the excess backing fabric and stitch it to the top back edge of the quilt, just below the binding. Hang your quilt...and enjoy!

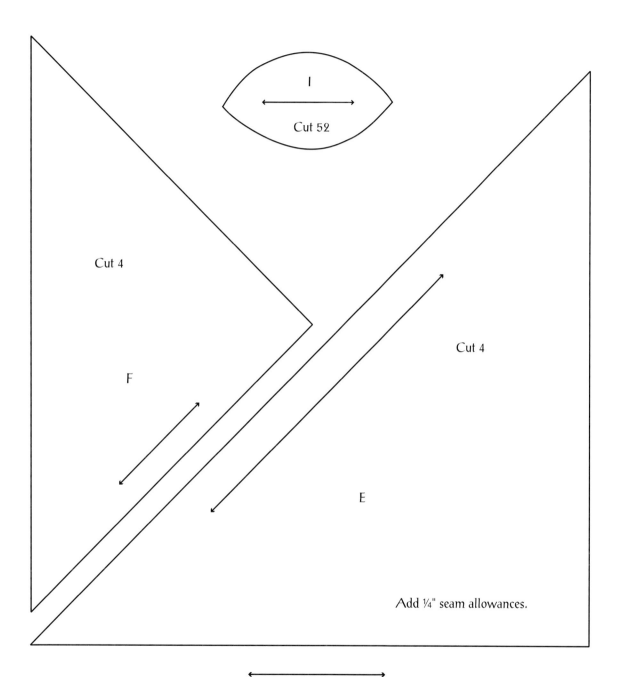

I
Cut 52

Cut 4

Cut 4

F

E

Add ¼" seam allowances.

Indicates straight of grain.

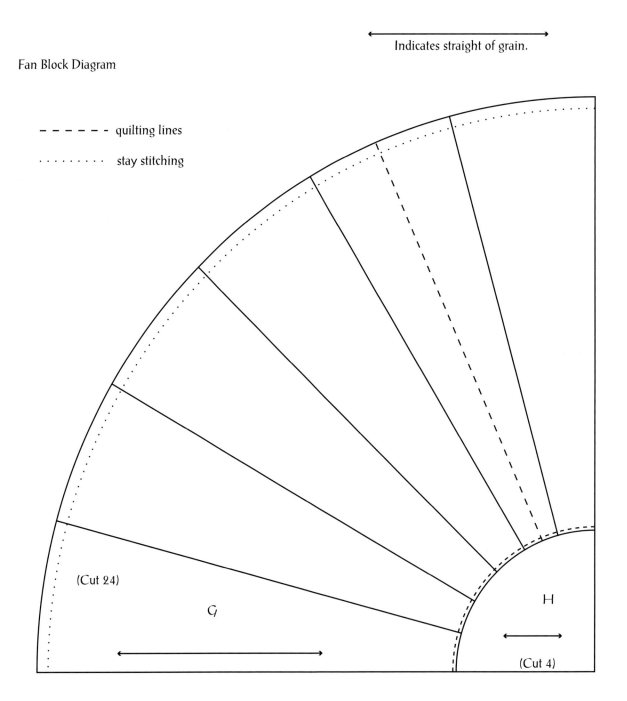

Fan Block Diagram

Indicates straight of grain.

– – – – – quilting lines

· · · · · · · · · stay stitching

(Cut 24)

G

H

(Cut 4)

Add ¼" seam allowances.

Star Block Diagram

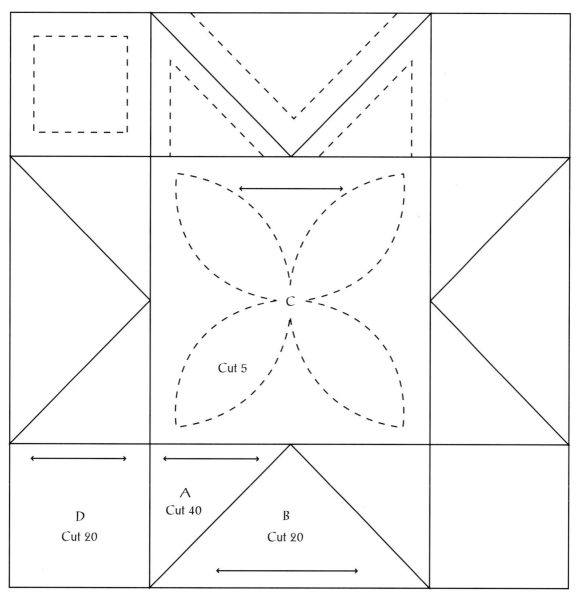

Add ¼" seam allowances.

Indicates straight of grain.

# _L_ITTLE _A_NGELS

### by Carol Doak

This small, 26" x 26", quilt of Little Angels combines a delightful pieced angel and a Four-Patch block. It will make the perfect gift for a quilting friend or angel collector.

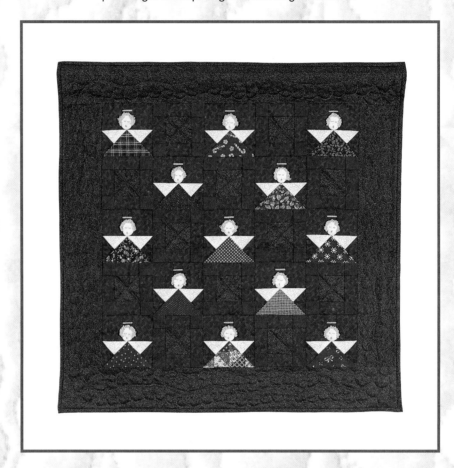

## FEATURED TECHNIQUES
Machine strip piecing
Pen and ink embellishment
Hand appliqué

## MATERIALS LIST

¾ yd. green for patchwork and border
½ yd. navy
⅛ yd. red
⅛ yd. white for wings
⅞ yd. backing
13 red and green scrap pieces each 3" x 6"  – angel dresses
1" x 18" gold for halo
2 skeins of yellow embroidery floss

Blue and red permanent pens
2" x 22" muslin for faces

This Little Angels quilt is comprised of a Four-Patch block and an angel block that alternate in a five block by five block setting with a 3" border.

### FOUR-PATCH BLOCK – 12 blocks

This 4" x 4" finished size Four-Patch block is rotary cut and machine pieced using a ¼" seam allowance. Two strip sets are sewn, cut into segments and combined to create the block.

# LITTLE ANGELS

Carol Doak, Windham, NH, is an award-winning quiltmaker, designer, teacher, and author. Carol's teaching has taken her to many cities across the U.S. and to Australia to share her "Tricks of the Trade." Her quilts have been widely published in books and national quiltmaking magazines. Carol is the author of **Quiltmaker's Guide: Basics & Beyond**, AQS, and five other books.

Carol Doak

## INSTRUCTIONS

### Strip Set #1
•From the red, cut 2 strips from selvage to selvage each 1½".

•From the navy, cut 1 strip from selvage to selvage 2½".

•Sew red/navy/red strips. Press seam allowances toward the navy fabric.

•True up one end and cut apart at 1½" intervals for a total of 24 units (Figure 1).

| | |
|---|---|
| | Red |
| | Navy |
| | Red |

Figure 1

### Strip Set #2
•From the navy, cut 2 strips from selvage to selvage each 1½".

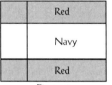

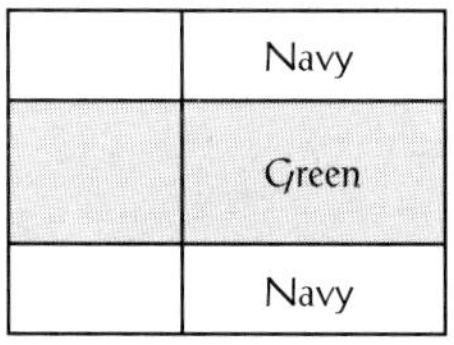

Figure 2

•From the green, cut 1 strip from selvage to selvage 2½".

•Sew navy/green/navy strips. Press seam allowances toward the navy fabric. True up one end and cut apart at 2½" intervals for a total of 12 units (Figure 2).

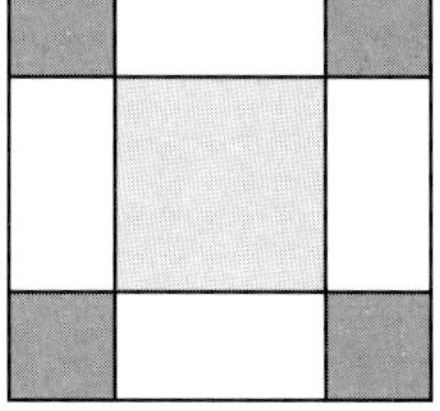

•Sew a #1 unit to a #2 unit and add another #1 unit to create the Four-Patch block (Figure 3).

### ANGEL BLOCK - 13 blocks
•Lower portion: From the navy, cut 7 squares 3¼" x 3¼" cut diagonally in both directions for a total of 28 triangles. (You will only use 26.)

Figure 3

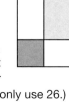

•From the white, cut 7 squares 3¼" x 3¼" cut diagonally in both directions for a total of 28 triangles. (You will only use 26.)

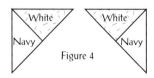

Figure 4

•Sew 13 units of both of the combinations shown in Figure 4.

•Cut 13 triangles, using template A for angel dresses from 3" x 6" red and green scraps.

•Tape template A to the corner of a rotary ruler. Place the ruler on each fabric scrap and rotary cut the 13 triangles as shown in Figure 5.

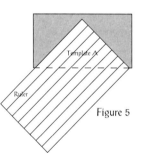

Figure 5

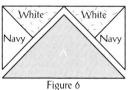

Figure 6

•Add the navy and white triangle sets as shown in Figure 6.

### Strip set #3
•Upper portion: From the navy, cut one strip 1⅞" x 18" and one strip 1" x 18".

•From the gold, cut one strip ⅝" x 18".

•Join the long sides of the 1" navy strip to the ⅝" gold strip and add the 1⅞" navy strip. True up one end cut apart every 1¼" for 13 units (Figure 7).

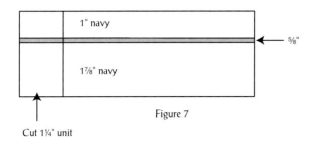

Cut 1¼" unit

Figure 7

•From the navy, cut 1 strip selvage to selvage and 2½" wide. Cut another navy strip 20" long and 2½" wide. Cut these strips into 26 pieces each 2⅛" wide.

•Sew these rectangular pieces to both sides of a #3 unit as shown in Figure 8.

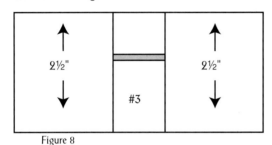

Figure 8

•Sew the bottom to the top of angel block as shown in Fig. 9.

•Following quilt picture, sew in rows (5 across and 5 down) in an alternating fashion.

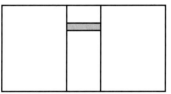

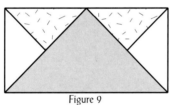

Figure 9

**Join Borders:**
•From the green, cut 2 pieces 3½" x 20½" (sides); cut 2 pieces 3½" x 26½" (top and bottom).

•Make a cardboard template for the angel face (Figure 10). Trace around the template on muslin fabric and cut out ¼" away from the line. Sew a running stitch in the seam allowance and place cardboard in the center. Draw thread to gather around cardboard and press. Carefully remove cardboard and position face on top of each angel body. Hand appliqué with beige thread.

Figure 10

•Use 3 strands of yellow embroidery floss and make loose French knots wrapping the thread around the needle about 3 or 4 times to make the curls for the hair. Mark eyes with blue permanent pen and mouth with red permanent pen.

•Sandwich and baste the quilt. Hand quilt or machine quilt as desired. Bind the edges.

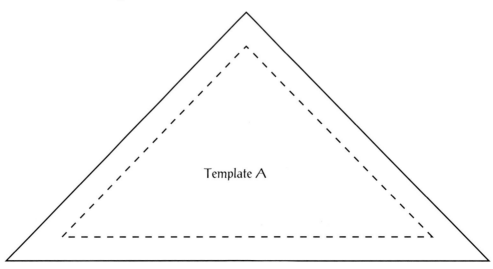

Template A

Includes ¼" seam allowance.

# My Two Angels

## WALLHANGING

### by Charlotte Patera

By cutting the fabrics simultaneously, switching the pieces, and appliquéing the edges, you can make your own My Two Angels wallhanging. It's sure to become a favorite holiday decoration.

## FEATURED TECHNIQUES
## Tandem reverse appliqué

## MATERIALS LIST

•Fabrics (substitute your own colors):
1 – 18¾" x 23" piece of plum (foundation)
1 – 9" x 22" piece of magenta (top layer)
1 – 9" x 22" piece of turquoise (top layer)
2 – 3½" x 23" strips of teal (border)
2 – 3½" x 24" strips of teal (border)
1 – 24" x 28" backing fabric

Thread – teal, magenta and plum
Batting – 26" x 30"
Quilting thread
Needle – sharp, 10, 11 or 12 as preferred
Embroidery scissors (sharp pointed)
Tracing carbon paper
Tracing wheel
Pins or basting thread

## INSTRCTIONS

•Position the pattern over the magenta fabric. Pin in place. Trace all of the lines.

•Remove the pattern. Pin the traced magenta fabric over the turquoise fabric, aligning the edges. Pin together. Cut on the edges shown as heavy lines on the pattern. This will result in five pieces of each color: the angel with wings, the space over her head, the two spaces on each side and the space at the bottom.

•Position these 10 pieces as shown over the foundation fabric. The pieces should butt against each other like a jigsaw puzzle. Pin or baste them in place. Omit the pins from the turquoise areas that need to be traced.

•Position the pattern over the left side and trace the

Charlotte Patera, Grasse Valley, CA, comes from a background of graphic package design and publication of ideas for national magazines. She is the author of **Mola Techniques for Today's Quilters**, AQS, and four other books. Intrigued by the "molas" of the San Blas Islands of Panama, she has made a thorough study of them and has frequently visited the islands. Much of her work is evolving her own appliqué methods based on these molas.

Charlotte Patera

details of the angel that are missing onto the turquoise fabric. Repeat this with the right side. Secure these areas with pins or basting.

•Working only one piece at a time, cut the edge of each piece on the traced lines and fold it under about ⅛". Fold and stitch, fold and stitch. Do not attempt to fold under the entire edge of one piece before stitching. Start stitching the folded edge under with small even stitches. Do not cut the whole design first. This will eliminate the need for detailed basting. The small parts will not shift position as long as they are not cut. Delay the cutting until you need to stitch each part down. Try to keep the spaces (channels) between the pieces even, about ¼". Figures 1, 2, and 3 show details for stitching straight lines, concave, and convex curves.

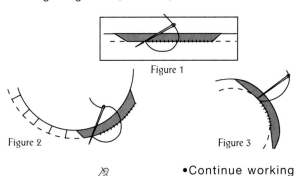

Figure 1

Figure 2

Figure 3

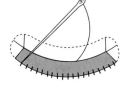

Figure 4

•Continue working this way until all parts are complete. To make the eyes and mouth, stab the fabric on the line with the point of your scissors and lift it away from the foundation. Make the cuts as shown in the detail diagram. Turn the edges under as shown in figure 4.

•When each piece is stitched down, press the whole work flat. Trim it so that the margins all around look

even. They should be about ⅝" in width. Appliqué has a tendency to draw up while working at your own tension so the margins may not be perfectly straight.

•Seam the two shorter teal strips to the sides of the piece and press. Stitch the remaining two strips to the top and bottom. Press. It is now ready to quilt.

•Quilt down the center of the channels that were formed between the pieces. Quilt by hand or machine as preferred. Quilt the facial details and the lines in the lower dress.

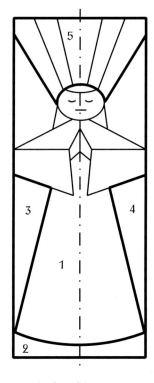

Reduced Pattern

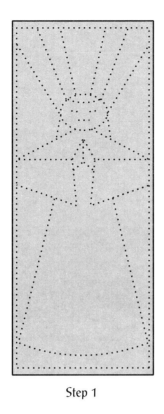

Step 1

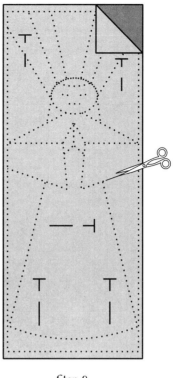

Step 2

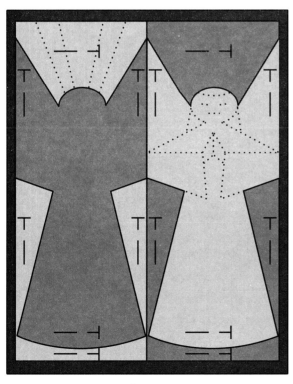

Step 3

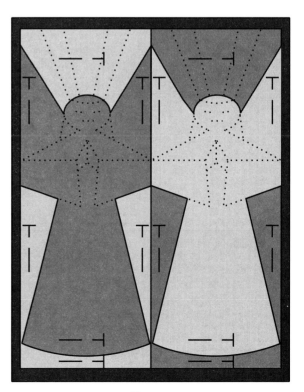

Step 4

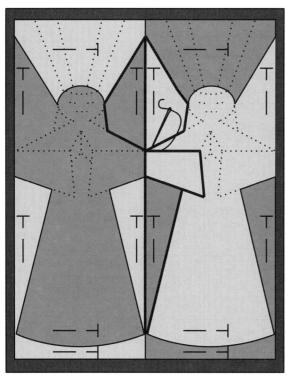

Step 5

Step 6

Step 7

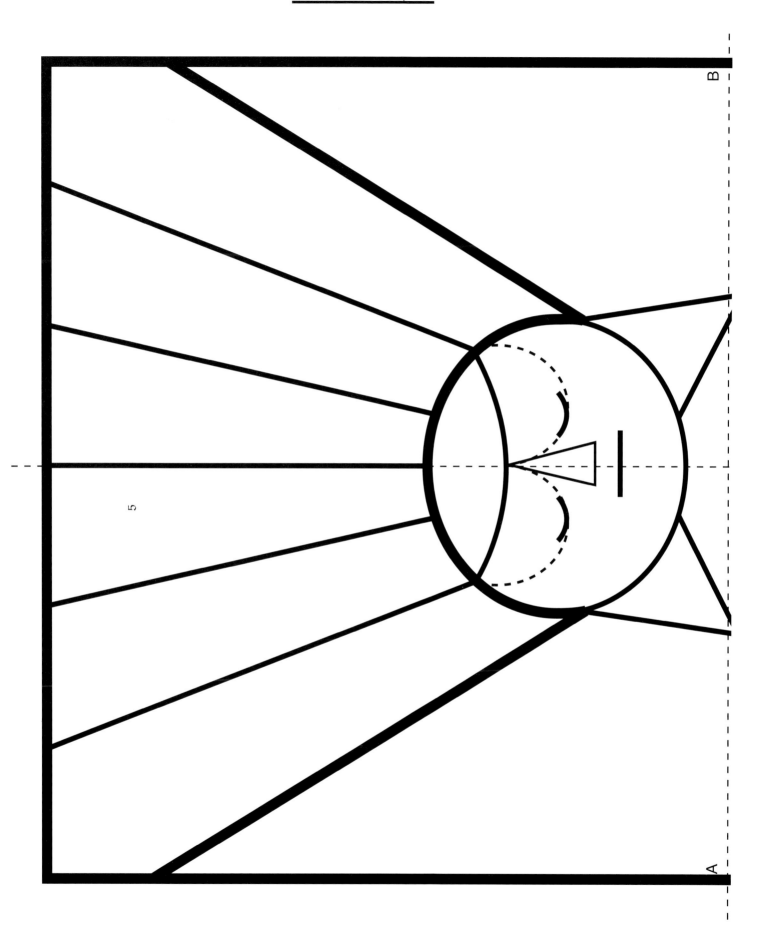

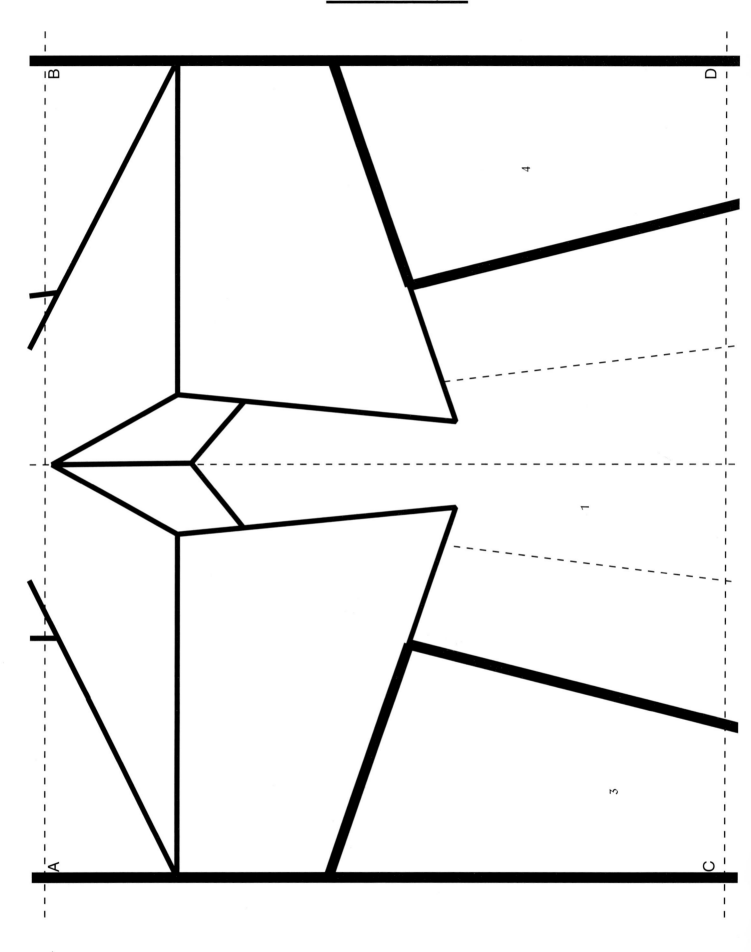

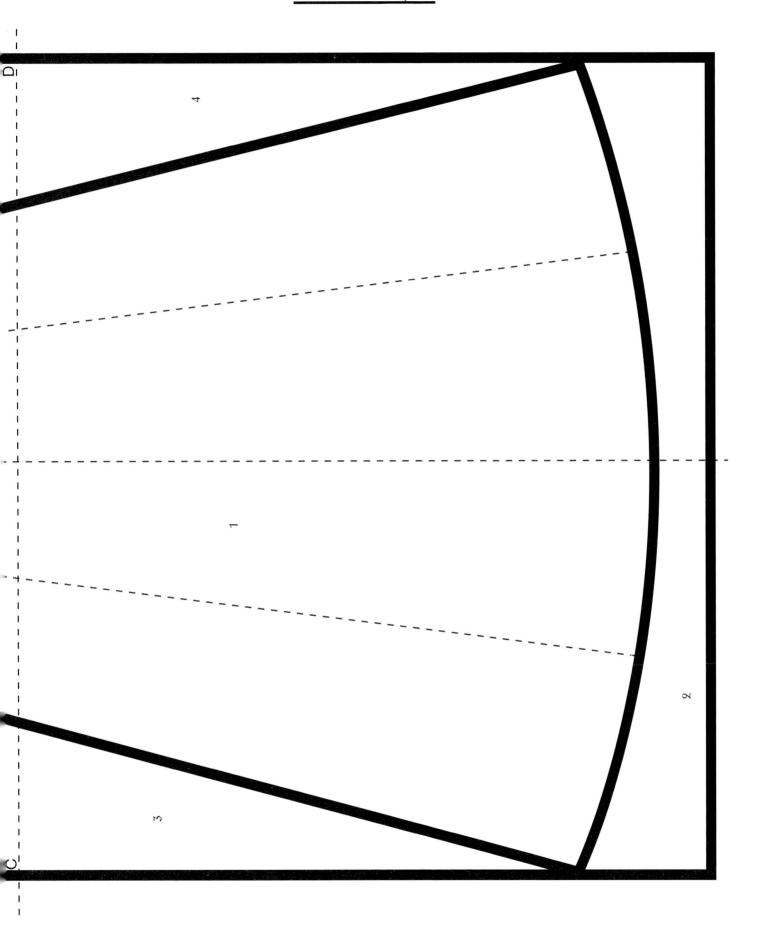

# NOEL BANNER

### by Anita Shackelford

This holiday wallhanging uses a variety of dimensional appliqué techniques and embroidery embellishments. The bow is made with gathered, stuffed, and unit-appliqué techniques. Embroidery stitches used are the blanket stitch, chain stitch, stem stitch, and straight stitch. Color blending lends depth and shadow to the evergreen. Stuffed berries add a dimensional touch to the piece.

## FEATURED TECHNIQUES
Gathered, stuffed & unit appliqué
Embroidery embellishments

## MATERIALS LIST

12" x 21" background fabric
½ - ¾ yd. border fabric (see * below)
8" squares of fabric for:
      letters
      holly leaves
      berries
      bow, if different from border
Small scrap of accent color for the bow
Embroidery floss: rusty brown; very dark, medium, and very light green to coordinate with fabrics
Sewing threads to match fabrics
Red quilting thread
Small amount of cotton for stuffing berries
Template material
Basic sewing supplies

*When choosing border fabric, consider if it has a directional design in the print or plaid. If the design runs lengthwise on the fabric, but is to be used horizontally as the gold line in this plaid, ¾ yd. will be needed. If the design is to be used vertically, only ½ yd. will be needed. Cut the top arch and bottom border first, then cut the bow from the fabric remaining.

## APPLIQUÉ

•Trace placement of the evergreen embroidery onto the background fabric. Mark placement of the other design elements as desired. I prefer to mark ⅛" inside shapes to be certain that the line will be covered.

**Leaves**
Only one template is needed for the holly leaves. Reverse as indicated by the pattern. Appliqué the holly leaves into place, beginning with the outside leaf and overlapping as shown.

**Bow**
•Cut the bow loops from the templates provided (Figure 1; pg. 88) rather than the pattern shapes. Cut the small accent color pieces as drawn on the pattern.

•Use the unit appliqué technique to add the small inside accent color to the bow loops. Turn under the lower edge of the bow which overlaps the small piece and blindstitch the two pieces together (Figure 2). You will see that after these two pieces are

Figure 2

Anita Shackelford, Bucyrus, OH, is an internationally-known teacher, lecturer, and certified judge, whose work combines 19th century dimensional techniques and fine hand quilting. She is the author of **Three Dimensional Appliqué and Embroidery Embellishments: Techniques for Today's Album Quilt**, AQS, and the designer of the RucheMark™ ruching guides. An award-winning quiltmaker, her work has been exhibited in shows across the country and published in many magazines.

Anita Shackelford

joined, turning the seam allowance around this whole unit will give you a perfectly smooth edge where these two pieces join.

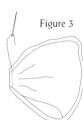

Figure 3

•Gather the center edges of the bow loops to a size to fit beneath the knot. (Figure 3).

Figure 4

•Appliqué the bow streamers into place, add the holly leaf in the center, and then position and appliqué the prepared bow loops.

•Appliqué the knot into place and add a small amount of stuffing before finishing the stitching (Figure 4).

### Letters
•The letters may be blindstitched or fused into place.

## EMBROIDERY

•Use a double ply of dark green floss to work a decorative blanket stitch around the edges of the letters (Figure 5).

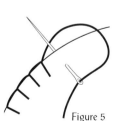

Figure 5

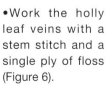

Fig. 6

•Work the holly leaf veins with a stem stitch and a single ply of floss (Figure 6).

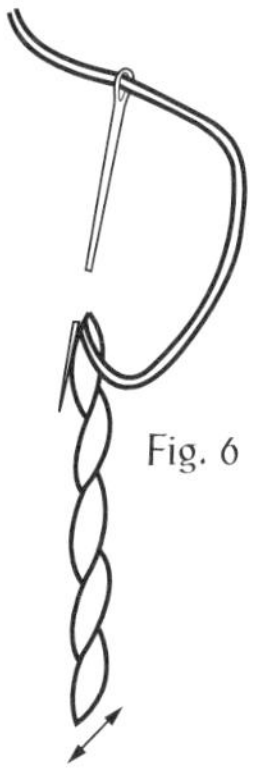

### Evergreen embroidery
•Use one ply each of rusty brown and dark green floss, in the same needle, to work a chain stitch (Figure 7) along the main branches of the evergreen. Use a single ply of medium green and a stem stitch to work all of the side stems shown on the pattern.

•The needles are added with straight stitches (Figure 8) after the main branches and stems have been worked. Use one ply each of light

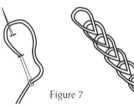

Figure 7

green and dark green floss in the same needle to add stitches along the stems, as shown (Figure 9). Notice that the needles grow in a "V" shape toward the tip of the stem. Be sure that the stitches are slightly random in size and placement and that some overlap.

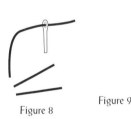

Figure 8

Figure 9

## BERRIES

•The berries are made in two sizes, using a 1" circle of fabric for the larger ones and a ¾" circle for the smaller. These sizes need no added seam allowance.

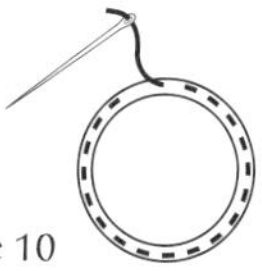

Figure 10

Figure 11

•Use quilting thread for extra strength and turn a tiny hem all around the fabric circle (Figure 10). Gather it slightly and stuff it with small bits of cotton batting.

•Pull to close the bottom and stitch it closed (Figure 11). To add the dimple, bring the needle up through the berry

Figure 12

and back down, leaving one stitch on top (Figure 12). Use the same thread to sew the berry into place.

## FINISHING

•Turn the finished block right side down on a heavy towel and press lightly. Mark the top arch and lower edge as drawn on the pattern and add ¼" seam allowance. Trim to shape. Make a template for the arch and add ¼" seam allowance all around. Stitch this top border to the piece. Cut a 2½" x 24½" strip for the bottom border. Stitch into place.

•Mark the radiating lines for quilting.

•Cut a layer of batting and a back to fit. Layer with the back right side up, the top right side down, and the batting on top. Stitch around the edges, leaving an opening for turning. Trim any excess seam allowance or batting, trim across the corners and turn the piece right side out. Hand stitch the opening closed and press the edges.

## QUILTING

•Quilt in the ditch around all of the appliqué, along the border and the background lines as marked.

Add a pocket shaped to fit the top curve. Leave a 1" opening at the top. Slip in a poster board cut to shape with a hole in the top for hanging (Figure 13).

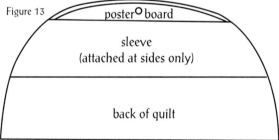

Figure 13

poster board

sleeve
(attached at sides only)

back of quilt

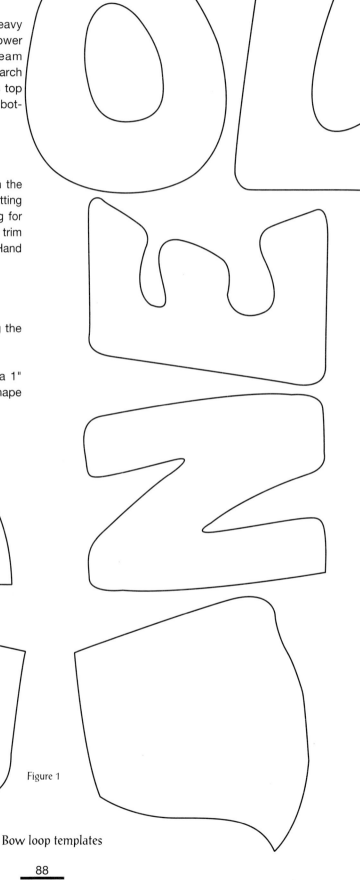

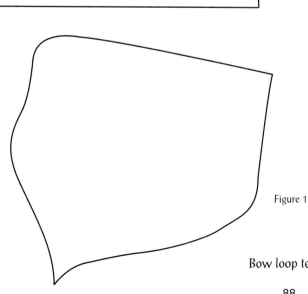

Figure 1

Bow loop templates

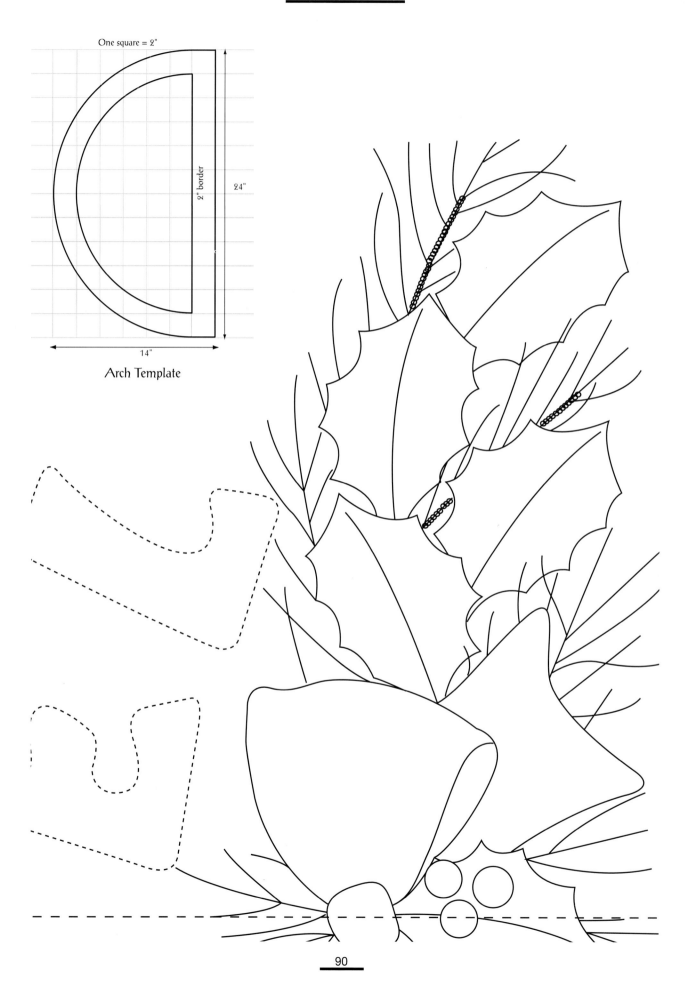

One square = 2"

2" border

24"

14"

Arch Template

# OPULENT ORNAMENTS
## FOR A CRAZY CHRISTMAS WALLHANGING
### by Karen Kay Buckley

Using scraps of cottons, velvets, polyester, rayon, and lamé, Karen Kay Buckley created Opulent Ornaments for a Crazy Christmas. You'll find it's quick and easy to do using machine techniques!

## FEATURED TECHNIQUES
Crazy patch piecing
Reverse appliqué

## MATERIALS LIST

Yardage requirements and supplies needed:
1 yd. for backing
1 yd. of green
¾ yd. of mulsin
Rotary cutter and mat
Plastic for templates
Scissors, both paper and fabric
Pencil
Ruler (small one for crazy patch and larger one for rotary cutting)
Fabric markers, be sure they are not permanent.
Four safety pins
Appliqué needle
Six silk pins

Glue stick water soluble
An assortment of scraps of cotton, velvet, polyester, rayon, lamé, etc. for the crazy patch areas. If purchasing, ⅛ yard pieces will be plenty. Scraps of lamé
3½ yds. of ribbon for the ornament and border area
Scraps of trims. Lace, ribbon, cording, and decorative threads.
Thread to match for piecing and crazy patch, green for reverse appliqué, thread to match trims for top stitching and metallic thread.

## CUTTING

•From your green fabric cut the following.
      Cut 4 squares 8½"
      Cut 4 strips 3½" x 44" for the border

Karen Kay Buckley, Carlisle, PA, has been quilting for 13 years and teaching for 10 years. She has over 200 quilts to her credit and has received many awards, both locally and nationally. Her first book, **From Basics to Binding: A Complete Guide to Making Quilts** was published by AQS in 1992. Her second book will be released by AQS in 1996.

**Karen Kay Buckley**

Cut 4 squares 3½" for the border corner units
Cut 3 strips 2" x 44" for the binding

•From your muslin cut the following.
Cut 2 squares 12⅛"
Cut 4 squares from muslin 8½"
Cut 4 squares 3½" for the border corner units

## INSTRUCTIONS

**Center Ornaments**

•Make a template of ornament A. Be sure to mark the line at the top center of the ornament on your plastic template.

•Take your piece of muslin and draw a line on the diagonal from one corner to the opposite corner. Place a mark on the line 1½" from the bottom edge. This will be the placement for the ornament.

•Trace the ornament shape onto the muslin square. The bottom of the ornament will be on the 1½" mark. The top of the template has a line for center positioning. Make sure that mark is on your center line. Trace around the shape. This can be done with pencil. This line will be covered so it does not matter if it washes out or not.

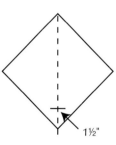

1½"

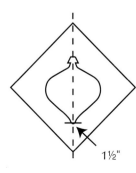

1½"

•Crazy patch over the ornament shape. Cut one piece of fabric with straight edges. You could start with a square or rectangular shape. Do not make this any larger than a 2½" square (1½" x 2½" pieces were used here). After the

shape is cut, chop off one corner. Five-sided shapes make crazy patch more interesting. All sides need to be straight. Refer to the diagram below.

•Place this shape some place close to the center of the drawn ornament shape. Pin this shape in place. We will refer to this as shape #1.

•Choose a second fabric. Place it right sides together, along any side except the chopped off straight edge of shape #1. Sew with a ¼" seam allowance from the edge of shape #1 to the other edge of shape #1.

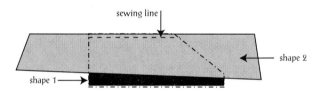

•Open shape #2 and finger crease the seam. Using your ruler, trace a line along the edge of shape #1, where it extends over shape #2. This will show you which portion of shape #2 is excess. Cut on the lines you drew to remove the excess.
*****If you would like to add a ribbon or trim to this seam now is the time. Heavy thread or cording can be couched over the seam. If using ribbon, top stitch with

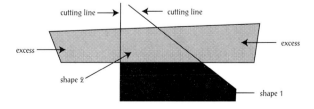

matching thread down both sides of the ribbon. If using lace top stitch along the edge of the lace with matching thread. Some lace has a seam allowance and can be sewn in the seam as the shapes are added. On some seams consider a decorative stitch with metallic thread instead of lace or a trim.

•To attach the remaining pieces, sew in a circular direction around shape #1. To sew shape #3, place it right sides together, along the raw edge of shapes #1 and #2. You will be sewing from the edge of shape #1 over to the edge of shape #2.

•Continue until the line you drew around the ornament template is covered. The crazy patch shapes should extend ½" beyond the edges of the ornament shape.

### Top of Ornament

•Trace a line ¼" from the straight edge of the ornament. With right sides together and the raw edge of the lamé on this line, sew with a ¼" seam allowance and then finger crease open. This will be the top of the ornament.

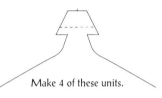

Make 4 of these units.

•To prepare for the reverse appliqué, trace the ornament shape onto the center of your green fabric square. This is done the same as the ornament you drew on your muslin, except be sure to use a fabric marker that will not be permanent, in case portions of it show. It will also be 1½" from the bottom center line.

•Center the green square over the crazy patch square. Using four safety pins, place one pin in each corner, through the green square and the muslin square. I prefer to place the pins in from the back side, so when I am sewing I do not get my thread caught around the pins.

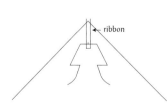

ribbon

•Glue ribbon on the center line for the top of the ornament. The ribbon should go from raw edge of the fabric to ¼" inside the top of the ornament. Do not stitch in place at this time.

•You are now ready to do the appliqué stitch. Use an appliqué needle and a single strand of thread that matches your green fabric. Work with six silk pins around the area you are appliquing. These will travel with you as you appliqué. You will be cutting the center ornament shape away, a little at a time. Do not cut it all at one time. The edges will start to fray, and it will be

more difficult to keep neat edges. Cut ¼" or less inside the line you drew. After you have sewn around the inside edge of the ornament shape, your crazy patch ornament will now show through the green fabric opening. As you are appliquing, stitch ¼" seam allowance for the ribbon under. After all of the appliqué is complete, top stitch the ribbon in place. From the back, trim the muslin square and the crazy patch edges down to ¼".

Sew the four ornament squares together.

### Crazy Patch Corner Units

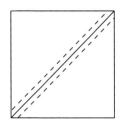

•Draw a line on the diagonal of the two 12⅛" muslin squares. Sew ⅛" from both sides of that line on each square. This will stabilize the bias. Cut the squares in half on the diagonal, giving you the four corner triangle base units.

•You will crazy patch over these triangles just like you did the ornament shapes. Sew a completed crazy patch triangle to each side of the four ornaments.

### Attaching the Borders

•Measure the four sides of your project. They should all be the same! If they are not, add all four measurements together, divide by four and use that measurement. Cut four green border strips 3½" by the measurement on your side. Be sure to include your seam allowance. (Mine measured 23¼" with seam allowance). Glue and top stitch ribbon down the center of each of these four strips. If you do not glue them before top stitching the ribbon can easily slide off center. Allow the glue to dry before you start to top stitch.

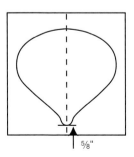

⅝"

•Make four border corner units as follows: make a plastic template of ornament B; center and trace this shape on your 3½" muslin and green squares. The bottom of ornament B should be ⅝" from the raw edge.

•Glue a single piece of fabric over the muslin ornament shape. This shape was not crazy patched. Pin a 3½" green square on top and complete the reverse appliqué. Satin stitch, with metallic thread across the top of each ornament.

•Sew the border units to the center portion by referring to the diagram below.

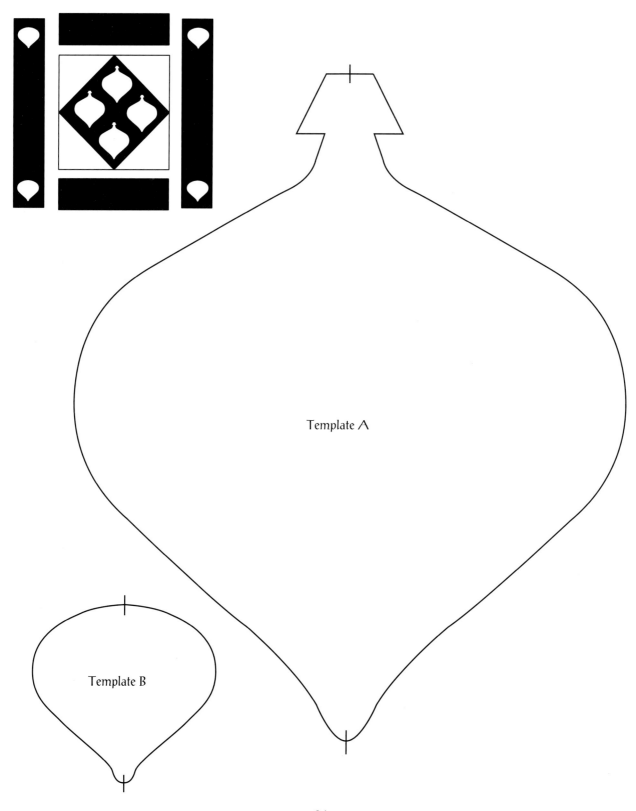

Template A

Template B

# PATCHWORK SEWING KIT

### by Jeannette T. Muir

The Patchwork Sewing Kit makes a perfect gift for the quilters and needleworkers on your gift list. How many can you make for your holiday bazaar or quilt show boutique? It's big enough to hold sewing supplies, and small enough to go everywhere.

### FEATURED TECHNIQUES
### Template making
### Piecing, by hand or machine

## MATERIALS LIST

Approximately 4" x 14" each of 3 light fabrics
Approximately 4" x 14" each of 3 dark fabrics
Approximately 18" x 22" (for hexagons and lining) of medium-color fabric,
8½" x 11" (scrap or muslin) for 1 interlining
8½" x 5½" for interlining of pocket
8½" x 11" batting
8½" x 5½" batting for pocket
3" strip of 1" Velcro®, or three, 1" squares
Template material, approximately 5" square
Sewing machine
Walking/even-feed/plaid matcher foot attachment
See-through ruler
⅛" paper punch

## TEMPLATE MAKING

Three templates, one hexagon "A," and two slightly different scalene triangles "B" and "C," are needed to prepare each unit as shown in Fig. 1. Be sure to mark circles labeled "a" for construction purposes as shown on templates B and C. Using a fine-point permanent marking pen, transfer the corners of each template to a firm, see-through plastic, by marking a dot. Superimpose the ¼" line of a see-through ruler on top of the dots, adding a ¼" seam allowance and solid cutting line. If desired,

Figure 1

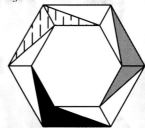

Jeannette T. Muir, Moorestown, NJ, is the author of the book, **Precision Patchwork for Scrap Quilts...Anytime, Anywhere**, AQS. Her quilt related involvement includes teaching, judging, designing and making quilts, entering competitions, collecting and restoring antique tops, and writing. She specializes in machine quilting, precision hand piecing, precision machine piecing, and working with scraps.

Jeannette T. Muir

connect the dots with dotted lines, which represent the stitching lines. Cut on the solid lines, and punch out the dots with a ⅛" paper punch.

## MARKING

•Placing the template on the wrong side of the fabric, transfer the dots to the fabric. Using a straight edge of the template, connect the dots to mark the stitching line. Three light and three dark "boomerangs" make up

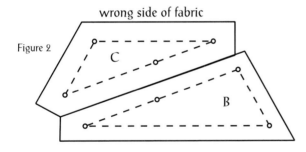

Figure 2

wrong side of fabric

each unit. To avoid losing small pieces, trace "B" and "C" on the same piece of fabric, as shown in Fig. 2. Cut apart when ready to stitch. Cut the hexagons from medium-color fabric.

## STITCHING

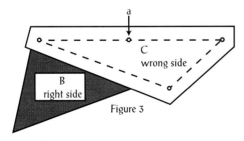

Figure 3

•Begin the stitching sequence by selecting any "B" and "C" combination, one light and one dark. With right sides together, pin, matching reference circles "a," and

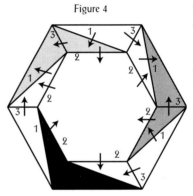

Figure 4

stitch seam from dot to dot, as shown in Fig. 3. Press seam toward the darker fabric. Continue stitching all matching pairs together. Next, stitch pairs to hexagon "A." Finger press dark triangles "C" toward the hexagon. Finger press the light triangles "C" toward the outer edge. The short ¾" seams are stitched last. Always stitch through only two layers of fabric. Fig. 4 shows the suggested numerical piecing sequence. The arrows indicate the direction in which to press the seams. Although the pressing instructions seem unusual, they will simplify the final assembly, and each unit intersection will fan neatly in alternate directions. Make seven full units as shown in Fig. 1. Cut two of the completed units in half, making sure to add ¼" seam allowance to one half. Discard the smaller portion. Stitch units together as indicated in Fig. 5. Template "D" is used to make the filler triangles at the tip and bottom. The corners are half of "D," as indicated by the dotted line. Reverse as necessary. The piece will measure approximately 8½" x 11".

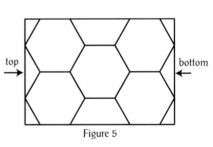

Figure 5

## QUILTING

Prepare the quilt sandwich for the patchwork piece,

batting, and interlining. Quilt as desired. Also prepare a sandwich for the pocket, using one lining piece, one interlining piece, and batting. Quilt as desired. Center and stitch fuzzy side of Velcro® 1" above lower (8½") edge of pocket.

## ASSEMBLY

Cut an additional lining piece 5½" x 8½". Stitch to quilted pocket, right sides together, using ¼" seam allowance, at the top edge. Turn lining to back and pin in place. Cut 1 lining piece 8½" x 11". On right side, center and stitch hook side of Velcro®, 1" from edge (8½" side). At the opposite end, run a row of stitching ¼" from the raw edge to facilitate turning and finishing. To assemble full sewing kit, pin pocket, right sides together with the quilted patchwork piece, matching corners and raw edges. Place full lining over top, right sides together. (Velcro® pieces should be at opposite ends.) Stitch, using ¼" seam allowance, rounding corners, and leaving a 5" opening at lower pocket edge. A walking foot will facilitate this process. Turn right side out and slip stitch opening by hand.

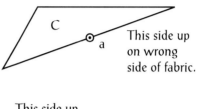

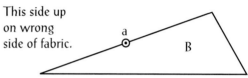

Add ¼" seam allowances.

Templates

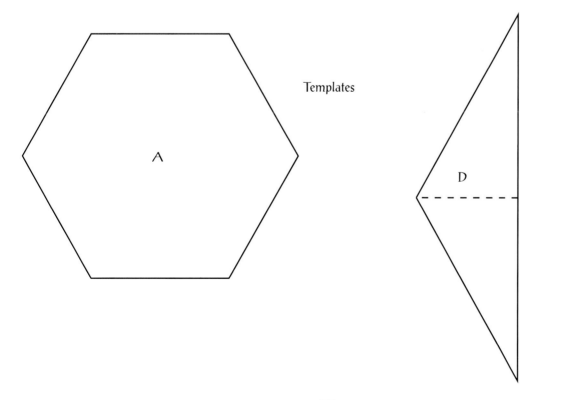

# PLAITED JEWELRY
## POCKET BAG

**by Shari Cole**

Weaving fabric tubes and stitching by machine makes Shari Cole's 20 pocket jewelry bag a gift that is easy to construct.

## FEATURED TECHNIQUES
## Plaited (woven) patchwork

The overlaps that form when fabric tubes are woven into a mat are a set of pockets waiting for treasures. With stitching to secure their open sides and bottoms, and a cover bag for security, these woven pockets become a convenient jewelry carrier for travel and storage. The option for hand sewing offers dedicated embroiderers a vehicle for a small masterpiece with decorative surface stitches, toggles, and tassels. Make a 20 pocket mat – 10 pockets on the front and 10 on the back hold rings and earrings. Large pins and brooches can be pinned to the outsides of pockets, and the cover bag protects them.

## MATERIALS LIST

⅛ yd. print fabric for horizontal strands
⅛ yd. solid or texture print fabric for vertical strands
12" x 21" plus 2" x 18" additional for bindings, complementary print for cover bag – must be attractive on both sides
10" zipper to match cover color

20" rattail, or silk cord, for pull and loop
Beads and threads for tassels optional
Weaving pinboard and pins – styrofoam, cork, or similar material – at least 10" x 9", slightly larger is more comfortable

## INSTRUCTIONS

**Making the pocket assembly**
•We interweave (plait) 4 horizontal strands through 5 vertical strands to make a cloth mat. The strands are tubes ironed flat. Some of these tube strands are not sewn closed along one side or end until the last stages of the project. All seam allowances are ¼" unless otherwise stated.

**Making Strands**
•For print horizontal strands

Hrz.    4 ⬚
        3 ⬚
        2 ⬚
        1 ⬚

Figure A-1

Shari Cole works internationally from Rotorua, New Zealand, writing, teaching, and making quilts, garments, and other craft art pieces. Her books are the result of 25 years' study of South Pacific art forms, her American quilting heritage, and independent experimentation. She encourages this exploratory approach through workshops and articles in quilting magazines. Her book, **Plaited Patchwork**, will be published by AQS in 1995.

Shari Cole

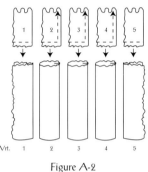

Figure A-2

cut 4 pieces 4½" x 10¾". Fold one in half lengthwise, right side out, and press. Call it horizontal 4. Fold the other three pieces lengthwise with wrong sides out. See Fig. A-1. Stitch along the long raw edge to make tubes. Turn and press the tubes with seams along the top. These are horizontals 1, 2, and 3. For solid vertical strands cut 5 pieces 4½" x 8½". Fold each of them in half lengthwise, wrong side out, and stitch across one end. Turn two of these right side out and press. Call them verticals 1 and 5. See Fig. A-2. Stitch the other 3 verticals lengthwise along the long raw edges as well. Trim the corners, turn, and press. Figure A-2 shows their position as verticals 2, 3, and 4. In plaiting we work from left to right and from near to far (bottom to top). This is why horizontal strands are numbered from the bottom, verticals from the left.

**Weaving the mat**
•Work with the edge that will be the top of the pocket assembly toward you. This allows you to use the near (bottom) edge of the weaving board to keep the tops

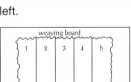

Figure A-3

of the first row of pockets even. Raw edges left at the far side will be trimmed even in finishing. Sewn tops of verticals go toward you, and folded edges of horizontals also toward you. Line up verticals 1 – 5 touching one another and with their sewn ends at the near edge of the weaving board (Fig. A-3). Long raw edges of verticals 1 and 5 face outward. Carefully remove verticals 2 and 4. Lay

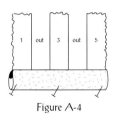

Figure A-4

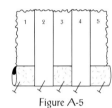

Figure A-5

horizontal 1 across verticals 1, 3, and 5 with its folded edge even with the edge of the weaving board and the ends of verticals Fig. A-4. Pin through horizontal 1 at verticals 1, 3, and 5. Its ends will extend slightly beyond raw edges of verticals 1 and 5. Replace verticals 2 and 4. Pin them as in Figure A-5. Now raise (fold toward you) verticals 1, 3, and 5. Lay in horizontal 2, with its folded edge toward you, as in Fig. A-6. Lower verticals 1, 3, and 5 to enclose horizontal 2. Pin through end verticals to secure the new horizontal. Fig. A-7 shows this movement and how it

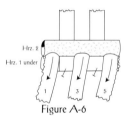

Figure A-6

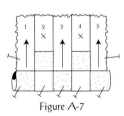

Figure A-7

makes a checkerboard pattern. Verticals 2 and 4 are marked X to show that they are the next strands to raise. This type of weaving we call plaiting. Complete the mat by plaiting. Pin the ends of each horizontal. The last horizontal, number 4, goes in with folded edge toward you, and long raw edge away from you. The finished mat looks like Figure A-8. Hand baste around the edges and across the two horizontal rows as the diagram shows. You can remove each pin as you pass it. The basting along the edge toward you holds the top row of pockets even, so should be more thorough than other basting.

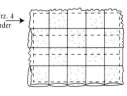

Figure A-8

**Sewing pockets**
•Trim any raw ends of strands that protrude beyond the raw edge that they cross. A clear ruler and rotary cutter

will help you to trim the ends evenly, keeping the mat rectangular and corners square. You may not need to trim it all. Figure A-9 shows the lines of stitching that secure the bottoms and sides of pockets. The mat is now turned so that the open tops of pockets face away from you. The edge where you started plaiting is now at the top of the picture. Stitch the bottoms of pockets across horizontal rows 1, 2, and 3 with a straight stitch close to the sewn edge (stitching marked 1). Though you can't see the edge as you sew across verticals, just aim for the next visible section of horizontal bottom edge. Your line will not wander off the edge hidden under the vertical.

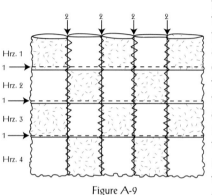

Figure A-9

Match thread color to solid fabric for all pocket sewing. Stitch the sides of pockets with a wide, open, zigzag stitch that catches the right edge of the vertical to the left with one swing, and the left edge of the vertical to the right with the next. Outside edges and the bottom of the horizontal row 4 will be secured by binding and by the cover bag, so you need not stitch them now. If you prefer to sew by hand, use an appliqué stitch, matching color to the solid fabric. Your stitches can hide under the edge of the strand you are securing, but horizontal lines (1) will show on the reverse. Plan to sew vertical lines separately, one line of stitching for each edge of each vertical. A further caution in hand sewing is to concentrate on not sewing the tops of pockets shut as you turn the mat over in pursuit of the edge you are stitching. An attractive alternate to machine zigzag is a machine embroidery stitch like Cretan or herringbone, not so dense as to stiffen the seam. This works best on simple prints where more detail adds to the overall effect. Finally, bind the right and left edges of the mat as you would bind a quilt. Cut 2 strips of the cover bag print 2" x 9". Fold them double lengthwise, right

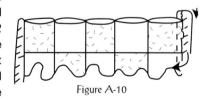

Figure A-10

side out, and press. Line up the raw edge of binding with the raw edge and strand ends of the left and right edges of the mat. The bottom of the binding is even with the bottom of the mat. The top of the binding extends beyond the top row of pockets. Stitch binding to mat. Turn the folded edge of binding to the other side of the mat and stitch by hand. Trim the excess at

the top to 1/2" and tuck it down before finishing the hand stitching. Figure A-10 shows the top portion of the mat in the binding process.

**Making the cover bag**

• Cut the front piece 12" wide x 9½" deep. Cut the back piece 12" wide x 11½" deep. Match one 12" raw edge of front and back, right sides together. Using ½" seam, sew with short stitches the first inch. Back stitch, then sew the next 10" with a long stitch which will be removed after the zipper is applied. Back stitch and finish with a short stitch. Press the seam open (Fig. B-1). On the inside (wrong side) of bag, pin the zipper face

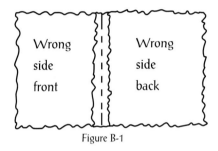

Figure B-1

down over the seam. Baste it by hand, folding the ends of the zipper tape under (toward the bag to conceal them) so they do not extend into the seams you will sew at the sides of the bag. Using a zipper foot, stitch around the zipper by machine. Stitching from the right side of the bag gives more control over the distance of stitching lines from the seam. Figure B-2 shows the assembly. Hand sew the folded ends of zipper tapes to the seam allowance, and ease the excess tapes under

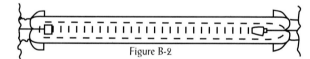

Figure B-2

to conceal them. On the right side of the bag, clip the stitching that holds the seam closed. Fold cover in half to find center; it should be approximately 1" from zipper. Crease to create line for couching the rattail or cord to make a hanger for jewelry bag. Mark the center of the creased line with a pin where the loop will be formed. Cut 16" of rattail or cord; couch by hand or machine, stopping to form the loop, and continue couching to the edge. Be sure to secure the base of the loop with several stitches. Trim any excess cord. See Fig. B-3. Fold the bag wrong sides together, matching

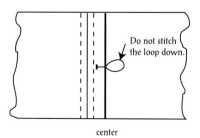

Do not stitch the loop down.

center

Figure B-3

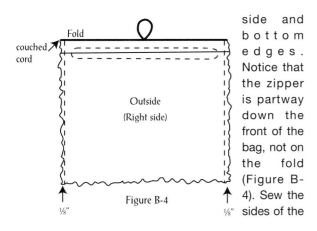

Figure B-4

couched cord

Fold

Outside
(Right side)

⅛"    ⅛"

side and bottom edges. Notice that the zipper is partway down the front of the bag, not on the fold (Figure B-4). Sew the sides of the

bag closed with a ⅛" seam. The bottom remains open. Turn the bag inside out and press the seams. As in Figure B-5 enclose the raw edges of side seams with a ¼" seam (French seam). Finally, turn the bag right side out and press the new seams.

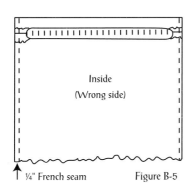

Inside
(Wrong side)

¼" French seam    Figure B-5

### Combining cover and pocket assembly

•Slip the cover bag over the pocket assembly, as in

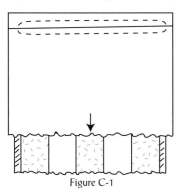

Figure C-1

Figure C-1. Open tops of pockets go toward the top (zipper end) of the bag. The bag is slightly wider than the pocket assembly to accommodate the French seams of the bag. Match raw edges of bag bottom to those of pocket assembly bottom and pin. Join all layers with a ¼" seam along the bottom (Figure C-2). Unzip the zipper. Pull the pocket assembly

through the opening, turning the bag inside out. Pull on the French seam to fully turn the corners. They will fold toward the bag along this bottom seam (Figure C-3). Tease the corner out with a pin to tidy it.

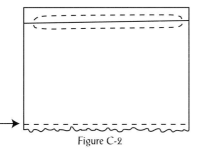

Figure C-2

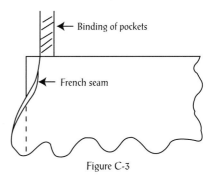

← Binding of pockets

← French seam

Figure C-3

Press the bag away from the pocket assembly. Using a zipper foot, stitch across the bag below the raw edges, enclosing them. Notice in Figure C-4 that the French seam rolls toward the bag at this stitching line, but remains free at sides and top of the cover bag. To pull

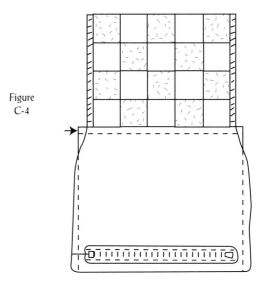

Figure C-4

the pocket assembly back into the bag, reach in through the open zipper and turn the bag right side out, smoothing it into place over the pocket assembly. Close the zipper and press the bottom seam. If desired, add small tassels or toggles to these bottom corners. They are decorative and also help in completely turning the bag right side out. Beads near the corner must be small so as not to interfere with turning the bag wrong side out for packing the pockets. A zipper pull is also helpful and attractive.

## EXTENSIONS

The cover bag affords security for escaping items and additional space for a larger piece of jewelry. You may prefer to sew snaps or button and loop closures to pocket tops and dispense with the cover. Simply bind the bottom edge of the assembly. By changing the initial width and length of strands, you can redesign the pocket plait to hold different sizes of jewelry, even different sizes within the same assembly. Why stop with jewelry? Use your imagination to find new functions for this form.

# POINSETTA TABLE RUNNER

### by Helen Kelley
Dress your holiday table with a reverse appliquéd poinsettia table runner, designed by Helen Kelley.

**FEATURED TECHNIQUES**
Reverse appliqué
Echo quilting

This table runner is made of two long, ribbon-like units. Each unit is reverse appliquéd to create half flowers. The finished half-flowers are then sewn together down the length to complete the design. Reverse appliqué is a technique by which the flower design is cut out of the background colored fabric (white) and then it is placed on top of the flower-colored fabric (red) and appliquéd to it. In this way, the flower color appears through window-holes in the white top fabric. You will prepare the background fabric by shaping the holes around cardboard templates using your iron and spray starch.

## MATERIALS LIST

⅓ yd. each of 2 red fabrics
⅓ yd. green
1 yd. white (+ additional for binding)
6" square of gold or yellow
16" x 45" piece of light-weight batt
22" x 28" piece of white posterboard (sometimes called tag board) of a weight that can be easily cut with a pair of paper scissors
Heavy duty spray starch
Basic sewing kit

## INSTRUCTIONS

•To make three templates, cut the piece of cardboard into three cardboard strips measuring 22" x 8". Mark the center of one long side of each cardboard strip.

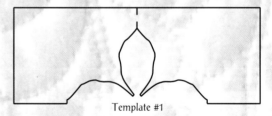

Template #1

Place the pattern (center mark indicated) on the edge of one piece of cardboard. Trace the flower shape indicated as #1. Turn the pattern over and trace it on the other side of the center dot to complete Template #1.

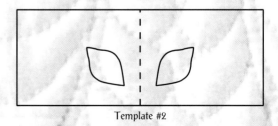

Template #2

Helen Kelley, Minneapolis, MN, has been a quiltmaker for much of her life. She spends a great deal of time researching, and has made an in-depth study of quilt history. Each quilt she creates is an exploration, using an "old" technique in a "new" way. Helen is the author of two books, including **Scarlet Ribbons, An American Indian Technique for Today's Quilters**, AQS.

Helen Kelley

•Repeat in like manner with #2 on the second cardboard piece, and #3 on the third piece of cardboard. Cut out the window-holes in the cardboards carefully and smoothly. Discard the holes.

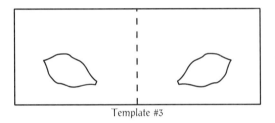

Template #3

•Cut fabric strips from selvedge to selvedge, 8" wide. 1 each of the reds, 1 green, 2 white.

•Cover your ironing board with a cloth to protect it from starch build-up. Place the first white strip on the ironing board. Place cardboard Template #1 neatly on top of your white fabric fitting against one end of it. Your template will perform best if you press with it, using it shiney side up. Push a pin through each of the four corners of the template into the ironing board to secure it. With a pair of sharp scissors, cut away the white fabric that is visable through the hole of the template, (leaving 1/4" seam allowance to be turned back over the edge of the template). Clip the fabric curves of the seam allowance to the edge of the clipboard template.

•Spray starch into a shallow cup. Dip your finger into the starch and dab the liquid onto the exposed seam allowance. Using the tip of a pointy iron, turn the damp seam allowance back over the cardboard edge. Hold the iron on the fabric until it is dry and holds its shape. After you have shaped the entire window-hole, go back over your edges, redampen and smooth any points and rough spots. It is not necessary to turn under the seam

allowance at the tip of the narrow strip between the petals. This area will be covered later with a yellow circle (Figure 1).

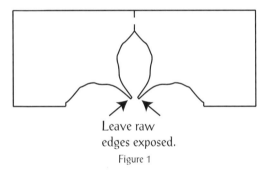

Leave raw
edges exposed.

Figure 1

•The fabric may adhere to the cardboard template. Loosen the edges of fabric with the tip of a seam ripper and remove the template.

•Place the template, same side up, on other end of the fabric in the same way. Shape it. Remove template.

•Place this "shaped" white strip on top of one red strip, matching the edges and with the raw edges of the windows down against the red. Pin together. Pin around the petal windows and appliqué them in place with white thread. Any uneven places can be neatened by dampening and turning with the tip of your needle as you appliqué.

•Press. Carefully trim away the excess red fabric on the back, leaving a ⅛" seam allowance. Set aside this red fabric for later use.

•Repeat with the second white strip, using the second red fabric.

•Place the first appliquéd strip on the ironing board, wrong side up. Place Template #2 (second petals) on top of it in the same way. Pin in place and shape these petals as you did the previous shapes. Using the left-over strip of the opposite red, place it beneath and appliqué. Trim.

•Repeat for the second white strip, appliquéing it to the opposite red remnant. Trim.

•Using Template #3, repeat the technique, this time appliquéing to a green strip of fabric to create leaves. Appliqué, press, and trim. To make the second set of leaves, adjust the green remnant to fill the leaf-holes. Appliqué and trim.

•Place the two appliquéd flower strips together, fabric edges and design matching. To complete the flowers, seam together down the length with a ¼" seam. Press.

•To make flower centers: cut one cardboard circle template and two yellow or gold fabric circles according to the pattern. Run a gathering thread around the outer edge of each fabric circle, and draw up the gathering

Figure 2

threads (Figure 2). Dab with starch and press. Remove template and make the second circle. Trim seam allowance to ⅛" to eliminate bulk around the edges. Apply to the center of each flower at the seam line, covering the raw points at the petal bases. Press. Trim away fabric from behind.

•Make two diamond templates according to pattern. Shape the larger with green fabric. Appliqué on top of seam line at the center of the piece (between the flowers). Press. Trim. Shape a smaller white diamond and appliqué it to the center of the green diamond. Press. Trim.

•Trim away selvedge ends. Straighten sides with your rotary cutter. Prepare for quilting. Quilt ¼" from edge of appliqué to camouflage show-through color. Quilt vein line in the center of petals and leaves. Echo quilt around the flowers in ¾" waves.

•Trim edges neatly and bind.

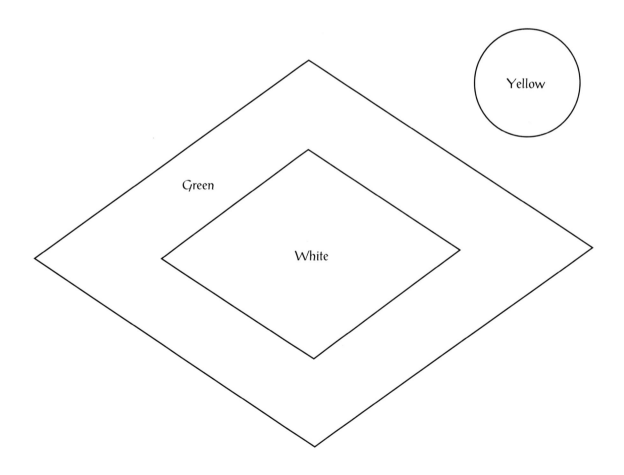

# POINSETTIA TABLE RUNNER

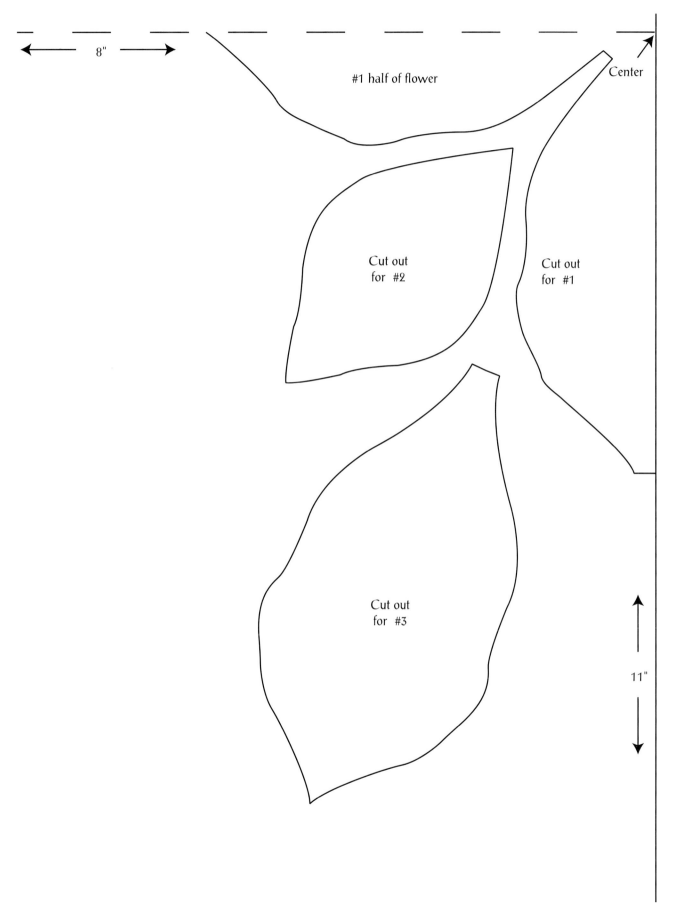

8"

#1 half of flower

Center

Cut out
for #2

Cut out
for #1

Cut out
for #3

11"

# QUILTED ANGEL & CHRISTMAS STAR
## BANNER

by Helen Squire

An angel, a Christmas star, and snowflakes are combined in this charming banner to softly share messages of the season.

## FEATURED TECHNIQUES
Machine Piecing
Hand quilting

## MATERIALS LIST

¾ yd. off-white satin
4 – 6" squares, red print
2 – 4" squares, dark green print
1 fat quarter (18" x 22") off-white fabric for background
4 – 2¾" x 17" strips of striped print
26" x 28" batting
1 yd. green solid fabric for backing

## CUTTING

•From satin, cut one 26½" x 38½" piece; from off-white background, cut 1 Template A, 8 each of Templates B, D, and E; from red, cut 16 Template C; from green print, cut 4 Template E; from green solid, cut 4 Template F; from stripe, cut four 2¾" x 17" strips.

## INSTRUCTIONS

### Christmas star

•Join off-white triangles (Template D) to the sides of 4 green (Template F) squares. Add red triangles (Template C) to each side. Make 4 units as shown in Figure 1.

Figure 1

Figure 2

Sew red triangle (Template C) to small off-white square (Template B), Figure 2. Press seam allowance toward red trian-

Helen Squire, Malvern, PA, is well known as the Dear Helen columnist and author of the AQS quilting design book series (**Dear Helen, Ask Helen, Show Me Helen**, and the soon to be released **Helen's Guide to Quilting in the 21st Century**). Since 1973 Helen has been a quilt shop owner, mail order source, teacher, lecturer, designer, consultant, and author. She teaches quilters and teachers at conferences nationwide.

Helen Squire

gles. Connect to the units made in Figure 1. The second and fourth rows will look like Figure 3.

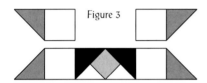

Figure 3

•Sew off-white triangles (Template E) to green print triangle (Template E), starting and stopping ¼" from edge. Leaving these seam allowances free makes it easier to press when the star is completed. Press seam allowances toward green triangle. Make four units as shown in Figure 4.

Figure 4

•Connect a corner square (Template B) and red triangle (Template C) made in Figure 2 to both ends of 2 units. These will be the top and bottom rows (see Figure 5).

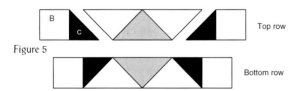

Figure 5

Top row

Bottom row

•Join rows one and two, four and five together (Figure 5). Match points and intersections and press toward the darker pieces as much as possible.

•Now connect off-white square (Template A) and two units made in Step 1 (Figure 6). Sew seam line to seam line, again leaving the seam allowance free from stitching. Press seam allowance away from center square.
•Pin the middle section Figure 6 to the top and bottom sections made in Figure 5. Join by sewing seam line to seam line. Press toward the darker colors.

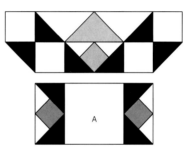

Figure 6

•Insert side sections; place sections of the green and off-white triangles along the sides of middle row (Figure 7). Sew seam line to seam line to join; *pivot to turn* Press seam allowance toward darker colors.

•Sew strips of striped fabric to edges of block, mitering corners. Appliqué block to satin centered 3½" up from lower edge.

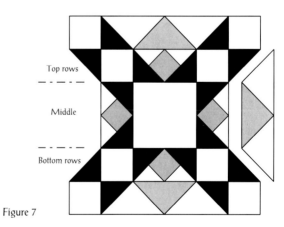

Top rows

Middle

Bottom rows

Figure 7

### Angel and snowflakes
•To make snowflake patterns, fold 9" square of paper in half, then into thirds. One sixth of the design is shown.

•Mark design of angel and snowflakes on upper portion of satin and quilt, using the color photo as a placement guide. A contrasting color of thread enhances the quilted design. Quilt along marked lines and in the ditch on seams of pieced block. Trim batting even with the top; trim backing fabric 1" larger than top at each edge. Fold backing ¼" to wrong side; slip stitch to front of quilt. Stitch a rod pocket to upper back for hanging.

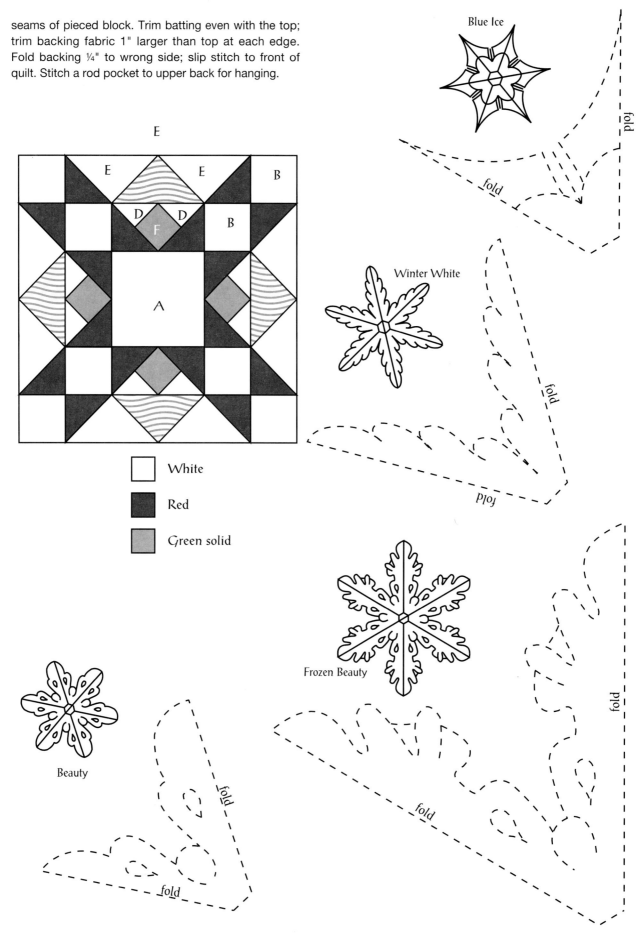

White

Red

Green solid

Blue Ice

Winter White

Frozen Beauty

Beauty

fold

Templates
Add ¼" seam allowances.

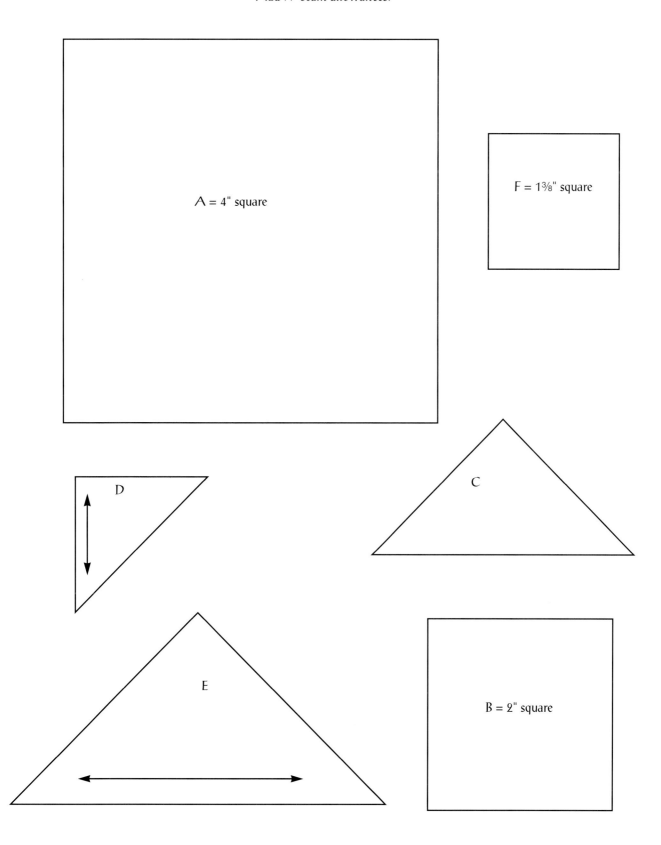

A = 4" square

F = 1⅜" square

D

C

E

B = 2" square

A

B

Diagram

From: …Ask Helen, More
About Quilting Designs, AQS

A

B

# ROSES IN DECEMBER

## by Faye Labanaris

Celebrate winter with a wreath of wire-edged ribbon roses, buds and holly leaves. A scalloped border of a Christmas print completes the piece. Gold metallic thread used to quilt the background adds a touch of sparkle to this charming gift.

## FEATURED TECHNIQUES
Wire-edged ribbon roses, buds, and holly leaves

## MATERIALS LIST

16½" square of ivory or white background fabric
½ yard border fabric
Fat quarter of a holly print for the wreath
1½ yards 1½" wide (size 9) of deep red or burgundy wire-edged ribbon for the roses
½ yard each of 1½" wide (size 9) of wire-edged ribbon, two different greens for leaves
Thread to match appliqué fabric and ribbon
Gold metallic thread

## INSTRUCTIONS

### Wreath foundation
•Fold and iron background fabric into quarters.

•Open fabric and trace heart wreath outline onto the background fabric with a pencil. Note where the two clusters of roses and leaves are located.

•Cut fat quarter of holly print into 1" wide bias strips. A total of 24" will be needed.

•Fold bias strips in half lengthwise, wrong sides together and iron.

•Place raw edge of bias strip onto the pencil-line

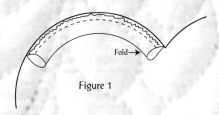

Figure 1

Faye Labanaris, Dover, NH, brings her love of flowers, teaching, and Hawaii into her quilts and classes. Faye's specialties included realistic wire-edged ribbon flowers, Baltimore album appliqué, and Hawaiian quilting. Her works have appeared in several books and magazines. Faye is the author of **Blossoms by the Sea: Making Wire-Edged Ribbon Flowers for Quilts**, to be released by AQS early in 1996.

Faye Labanaris

wreath. Position strip so that raw edges of the strip face the outside of the wreath and the folded edge of the bias strip points toward the inside of the wreath. See Figure 1.

•Stitch the strip in place, ⅛" from the raw edge, using a tiny running stitch. You may use a sewing machine for this stitching.

•Turn bias strip over the sewing line. Pin in place and sew down with an invisible stitch. Wreath foundation is complete. Make leaves next.

**Wire-edged Ribbon Leaves**
•Cut green ribbon into 6" lengths. Each strip will make a pair of holly leaves. Leave the wire in place.

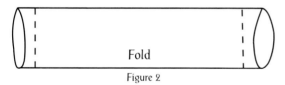

Fold

Figure 2

•Fold ribbon in half lengthwise. Stitch the open ends closed with a ⅛" seam (Figure 2). This step may be done on a sewing machine to speed up the process.

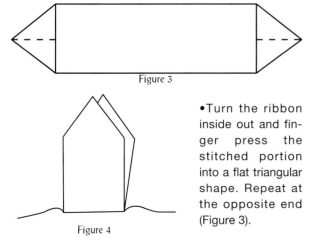

Figure 3

Figure 4

•Turn the ribbon inside out and finger press the stitched portion into a flat triangular shape. Repeat at the opposite end (Figure 3).

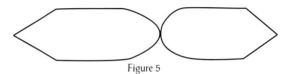

Figure 5

•Fold ribbon in half, matching the two triangular tips (Figure 4). Slip a thread or wire through the folded end and twist tightly to form a gathered center (Figure 5). If using thread, knot securely.

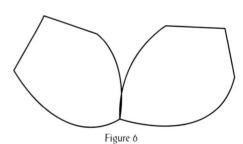

Figure 6

•Spread open leaves and arrange in a pleasing manner where indicated on diagram (Figure 6). You will make 6 pairs of leaves. Rose cluster uses 4 pairs and lower cluster uses two.

**Wire-edged Ribbon Roses**
•Remove and save 24" of ribbon for 8 rose buds. Use remainder to make the rose.

Figure 7

•For a Full Blown Rose, use 18" to 36" of wire-edged ribbon of any width. Begin to gather the ribbon by exposing about 1" of wire from each end of one edge only of the ribbon. Be careful not to pull the wire. Sim-

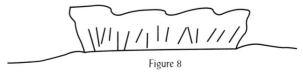

Figure 8

ply hold the wire and gently push or slide the ribbon toward the center section.

•Work both edges alternately until the ribbon is gathered tightly, without forcing, on one edge of the wire.

•Secure the ribbon gathers from escaping by wrapping the wire around itself and the salvage edge a couple of times. See Figure 9.

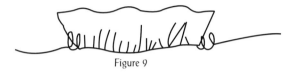

Figure 9

•Secure or anchor the gather on both ends of the gathered ribbon. Do not cut off the excess wire, yet.

•To form a center bud and stem handle, push the ungathered (top) edge of the ribbon down to the gathered (bottom) edge (Figure 10). Squeeze together about 1 inch of end ribbon.

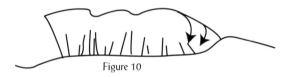

Figure 10

•Wrap the excess wire around the squeezed ribbon to form a center bud and stem/handle (Figure 11).

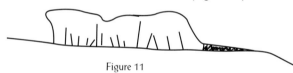

Figure 11

•Begin to roll the stem/handle along the gathered ribbon bottom edge about two revolutions. At this point you may stitch the bottom rows together to prevent slippage.

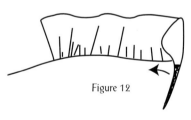

Figure 12

•Now begin to spiral the gathered ribbon length up and away from the rose stem (Figure 12). The rose will now begin to grow or bloom!

•Turn the rose upside down and secure each row to the previous row with a whipstitch. The rows should be about ⅛" to ¼" apart. The further apart the rows are the larger your rose will "grow."

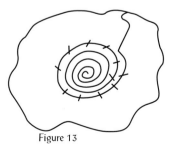

Figure 13

•Fold the raw edge of the ribbon under and stitch to the back of the rose (Fig-

ure 13). Realistic leaves cut from fabric may be used as an accent or add ribbon leaves. Rose is attached to background with a few hidden stitches through the rose. Petals may be stitched into place with a couple of hidden stitches to achieve the desired look.

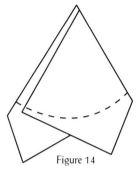

Figure 14

### Rose Buds
•Each rose bud requires 3 inches of 1½" wide wire-edged ribbon.

•Fold ribbon into a triangle with overlapping folds of the ribbon. Trim excess ribbon from the bottom edge, forming a slight curve (Figure 14).

•Using double thread, stitch a row of running stitches ⅛" up from the bottom edge (Figure 15). Pull tightly, and "gather ye rosebuds!" Secure with a knot. Repeat the process until all eight rose buds are completed.

Figure 15

### Wreath Construction
•The upper right "rose corsage" requires 4 pairs of ribbon leaves, 6 rose buds and one rose.

•Position rose in an off-centered position on the inner portion of the upper right section of the bias wreath.

•Position the leaves in a pleasing arrangement under the rose using various shades of green.

•Position the rosebuds under the v-section of the leaves.

•When the arrangement is pleasing, pin all the leaves and buds in place. Remove the rose. Tack the leaves and buds in place with matching thread and invisible stitches. Position and sew the rose in place with hidden stitches throughout the folds and gathers. Arrange the petals to your liking and tack in place with hidden stitches.

•Complete the lower left leaf and bud garnish with the remaining two pairs of leaves and two buds.

### Border and Quilting
•Appliqué scalloped border in place.

•Using the center fold lines as a guide, mark radiating lines outward. A v-shape intersection will occur at the fold lines.

•Quilt these lines with gold metallic thread for a touch of sparkle. Sign and date. Enjoy!

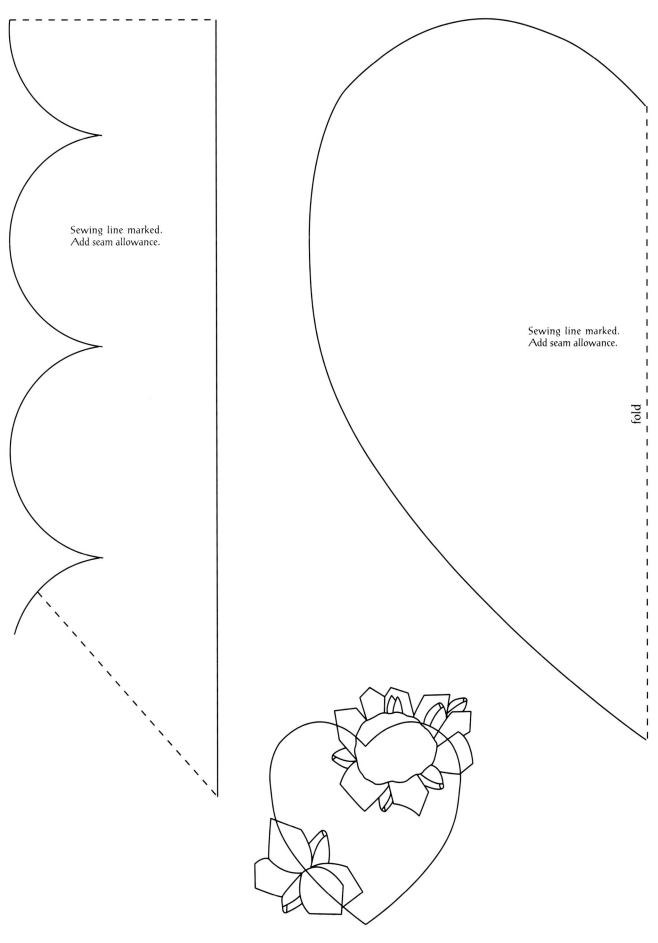

Sewing line marked.
Add seam allowance.

Sewing line marked.
Add seam allowance.

fold

# SCHERENSCHNITTE HOLLY & MISTLETOE

## A 4-BLOCK MINIATURE QUILT

*by* **Linda Carlson**

Scherenschnitte Holly and Mistletoe, a 4-block miniature quilt, uses paper cutting method of block preparation. Only four blocks are needed to complete this 30" square wallhanging.

### FEATURED TECHNIQUES
Scherenschnitte (paper folded) patterns
Hand appliqué
Stuffed berries
Embroidery embellishment

## MATERIALS LIST

1½ yds. green for background and borders
½ yd. red for scherenschnitte holly
5" x 5" square, scrap white for 12 mistletoe berries
Scrap pieces of batting for berries
4 mistletoe type leaves cut from "cheater" fabric
36" square batting
Threads to match fabrics
Scrap pieces of brown and/or green embroidery thread

Basic sewing supplies

## CUTTING

•From background fabric, cut:
    4 – 10½" squares
    2 – 5½" x 30½" borders
    2 – 5½" x 20½" borders

•From remainder of fabric cut binding to measure 2" x 130"

Linda Carlson, Mexico, MO, has been fascinated since the 1980's by the large 4-block quilts popular from 1830 – 1870. She lectures and teaches classes nationally, based on her book, **Roots, Feathers & Blooms: 4-Block Quilts, Their History & Patterns**, AQS. In 1995 Linda was a featured lecturer at the Smithsonian Institute's symposium, "What's American About American Quilts!"

Linda Carlson

•From scherenschnitte holly fabric, cut:
    4 – 10½" squares

•From scrap white fabric, trace around a dime to make 12 berries.

## INSTRUCTIONS

•Pre-shrink all fabrics and repeat instructions for all four blocks. Finger press background block in fourths to find center of block. Finger press red square in fourths to find center of block then finger press diagonally both ways. Center and trace scherenschnitte holly pattern onto red fabric. Only trim away the seam allowance on the outside edges of the pattern for now. Cutting line should be a healthy ⅛" from outside edge of marked line. Pin center of scherenschnitte holly to center of green background block and four corners. Using long basting stitches, baste along finger pressed folds.

•Starting at center, about two inches at a time, trim seam allowance to ⅛" and appliqué to block using the needle turn method. Repeat for remaining center sections. Needle turn appliqué the outside edges of the pattern last.

•When all four blocks are appliquéd, sew together to form a square. Add shorter border strips to top and bottom of square. Finish the top by adding the longer border strips to sides.

•Appliqué the four leaves to the corners of the top. Baste about ⅛" inside berry circle. Stuff with scrap pieces of batting and pull threads tightly so berry is small and round. Repeat for remaining berries, then sew three berries to within 1" to 1½" from lower parts of leaves. Using three strands of floss, embroider stems with a chain stitch to attach berries to leaves.

•To draw slanted quilting lines on the borders, start at the top left corner. Align ruler from outside edge of border to the corner of the four block square. Draw a line. Draw one more line on each side of it ¼" away. (See Figure 1.)

•Repeat instructions for lower right corner.

•At a 45 degree angle, measure ¾" away from last drawn line on the top border. Draw another line. From here you may use one of two marking methods.

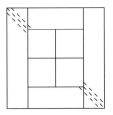

Figure 1

1. Continuing with 45 degree angle, draw two more lines ¼" apart. Repeat ¾" space between the sets of three lines.

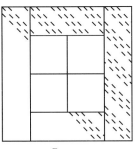

Figure 2

2. From first line, draw a 45 degree angle line ½" away and use ¼" masking tape to mark the inside ¼" line and quilt along it. Continue to draw lines across the top border using one of these methods consistently. It is important to check the 45 degree angle often. When you approach the outside edge of the top right block, you may draw lines on the right side border as you mark the top border.

•Repeat instructions for the lower right corner working on the right side border towards the lines marked on the top border.

Continue marking lines on the bottom right corner towards the bottom left border edge, then from the top left corner down the left side towards the bottom border. Remember to constantly check the 45 degree angle.

Baste backing, batting, and top together. Quilt and bind with 2" double fold binding. Make and sew a 2" finished folded sleeve to the back for hanging.

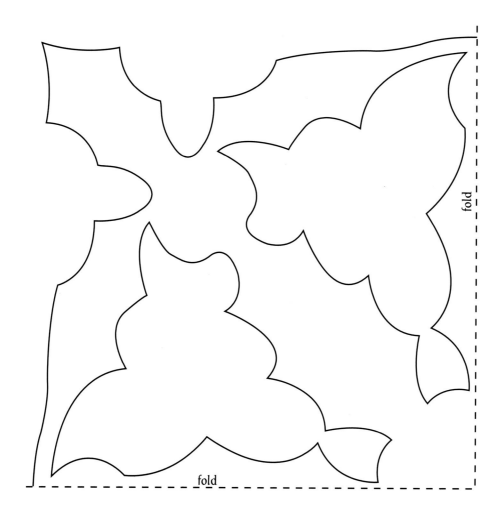

fold

fold

# Scrap Bag
## STAR QUILT
### by Mary Stori

Inspiration for this quilt came from a cross-stitch star pattern discovered while searching for an uncommon pattern to make a one-patch charm Christmas quilt. Since Mary Stori's enthusiasm was greater than her patience for collecting charm squares, a number of the scrap fabrics were repeated. Read through pattern instructions before beginning.

## FEATURED TECHNIQUES
### Machine piecing

## MATERIALS LIST

625 – 3" x 3" scraps in various prints from the following combination of colors:

> 288 – beige
> 96 – dark brown/black
> 80 – dark green
> 64 – red
> 48 – medium green
> 32 – light-medium green
> 17 – light green

**Borders & Binding**

2 yds. solid red – cut into:

> 4 – 2½" x 63" strips (borders)
> 20 – 2½" x 2½" patches (9-Patch border units)
> 9 yds. – 2½" wide (double binding)

2 yds. solid dark green – cut into:

> 8 – 2½" 63" strips (borders)
> 16 – 2½" x 2½" patches (9-Patch border units)

**Backing:** 4½ yds.
**Batting:** 80" x 80"

## INSTRUCTIONS

•Piece 64 Nine-Patch blocks (finished block size 7½") following the color-coded star diagram. NOTE: It will be necessary to add an additional row, consisting of beige and dark brown/black squares, to each of the 8 outside right vertical and 8 bottom horizontal blocks to complete the design (Figure 1).

•Join the blocks together to create 8 horizontal rows, each containing 8 Nine-Patch units, using the diagram as a placement guide. Sew the rows together. The star sections should now measure 63" square.

•Stitch the 4 Nine-Patch border blocks together, using 5 solid red and 4 solid green (2½" x 2½" pieces) for each block.

Mary Stori, Prospect Heights, IL, is a lecturer, teacher, author, designer, and quilter whose work has appeared and won awards in numerous national shows. Her articles have been published in several national magazines, and her book, **The Stori Book of Embellishing**, AQS, guarantees inspiration! Traveling across the country to present lectures, workshops, and fashion shows of her wearables keeps her motivated.

Mary Stori

•Sew a green border strip lengthwise to each side of a red border strip. Repeat for remaining 3 borders. Stitch two of the pieced borders to the quilt top, at opposite ends. TIP: sew the entire center star portion of the quilt together before cutting the border strips. If necessary, adjust the length of the border strips to match your pieced star.

•Join a Nine-Patch border block to each short end of the two remaining pieced borders. Sew to the quilt top.

•Baste batting and backing to completed quilt top. Quilt as desired. Bind in red to finish.

•OPTIONAL: The star shape could be made more pronounced if beige and dark brown/black half square triangle patches replaced the brown/black square at the tip of each star point.

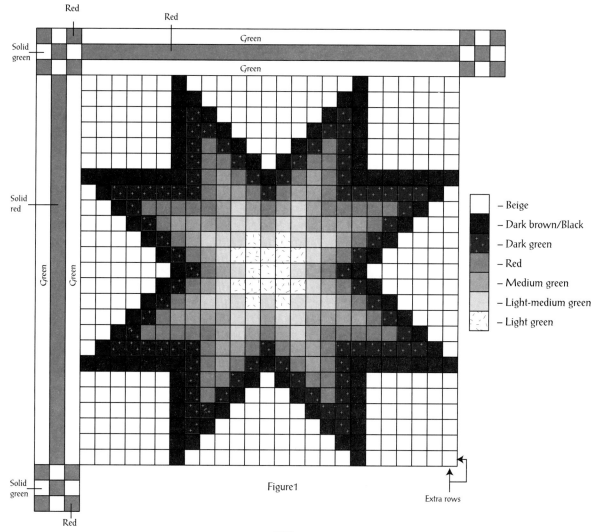

Figure 1

– Beige
– Dark brown/Black
– Dark green
– Red
– Medium green
– Light-medium green
– Light green

# SPIKE AND ZOLA

## CELEBRATE CHRISTMAS WALLHANGING

**by Donna French Collins**

Spike and Zola celebrate Christmas in this Christmas tree shaped wallhanging. Donna French Collins shares directions for needle turn appliquéing the flamingos in this fun project.

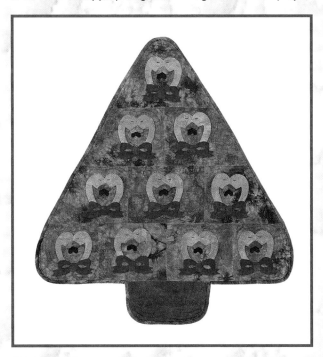

### FEATURED TECHNIQUES
### Needle turn appliqué

## MATERIALS LIST

1 yd. green
¼ yd. flamingo color
¼ yd. red for bows
⅛ yd. pink
⅛ yd. brown
⅛ yd. black
Black floss for eyes

## INSTRUCTIONS

**Appliqué**

•Enlarge the tree background using the grid method or take to your local photocopy shop and enlarge 400%. Spike, Zola, and the bow templates are shown full size.

•Measure blocks and borders and add ¼" seam allowance to all. Cut background fabric for blocks and borders and add ¼" seam allowance to all. Cut back-ground fabric for blocks and borders. You may wish to add ½" all around and trim the blocks to fit after you finish the appliqués.

•Tape pattern on light box or to a window, center background fabric on pattern and trace with a mechanical pencil. Use a light touch and trace pattern just inside pattern lines. This makes it easier to cover pencil lines when appliquéing. Remove fabric.

•Place fabric for appliqué on the light box or window. Trace just outside the pattern lines with a white chalk pencil. These lines should brush off after appliqué is finished. Cut out each piece adding a ⅛" to ¼" seam allowance.

•Work the appliqués from the background to the fore-ground. Pieces which are under another piece should be appliquéd first.

**Needle Turn Appliqué**

•In needle turn appliqué, your needle is your tool.

Donna French Collins, Bridgeport, NY, has been quilting since 1985 and currently teaches appliqué. Her prize-winning quilts have been exhibited in many shows and published in a variety of quilting books and magazines. Donna is the author of **Spike & Zola: Patterns Designed for Laughter...and Appliqué, Painting or Stenciling**, AQS, and currently designs her own line of patterns.

Donna French Collins

Place appliqué piece on background, matching lines on appliqué to lines on background fabric. Pin in place. Using thread to match appliqué fabric, knot thread, and start at a point or the straightest edge of appliqué piece. Turn under seam allowance, bring needle up through background and fold of appliqué fabric, while holding appliqué in place with tip of thumb or nail. With knot on back of background fabric, now you will only work from the top of the fabric. Insert needle just behind first stitch (through background fabric only), make a small stitch, come up through both background and fold of appliqué piece. With your needle, turn under seam allowance a little at a time, insert needle just under last stitch through background and up through both background and fold of appliqué, continue around piece in this manner. Leave seam allowance flat under covered edges.

## Finishing

•Sew blocks together according to pattern layout and press entire piece carefully from back.

•Layer top, batting, and backing, cut to fit and baste securely.

•Quilt around each appliqué piece using echo quilting. See quilting diagram.

•Bind with a 2" bias strip folded in half. Add a tab at the top for hanging and a 1½" sleeve to insert a dowel to keep the tree straight at the bottom.

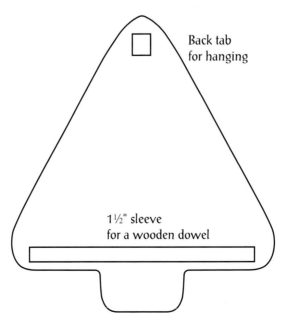

Back tab
for hanging

1½" sleeve
for a wooden dowel

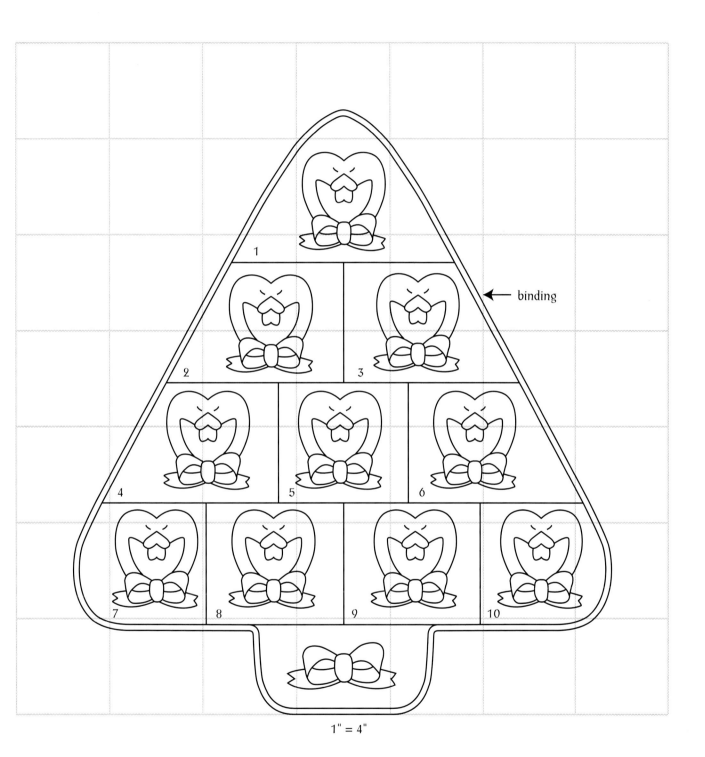

binding

1" = 4"

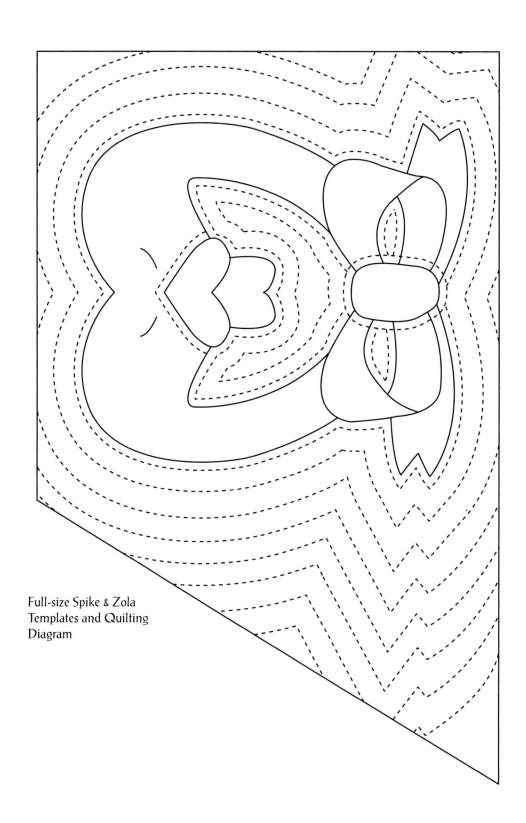

Full-size Spike & Zola
Templates and Quilting
Diagram

# STARRY CHRISTMAS NIGHT

## WALLHANGING

### by Eileen Thompson Lehner

Starry Christmas Night was designed by Eileen Thompson Lehner on a computer, Version 2.0 of The Electric Quilt software. Imagine getting to preview your quilts and making changes without ripping a single seam. What you see is what you stitch! Hand-dyed fabrics were chosen to depict stars in the night sky over Bethlehem.

**FEATURED TECHNIQUES**
Computer generated design
Machine piecing
Machine quilting

## MATERIALS LIST

Approximately 4 yds. total in fat quarters of 9 blues/purples and 6 golds. (hand-dyed American Beauty fabrics were used in sample).

Small pieces of additional colors for accents, such as light strips in the large central star.

1 yd. background for star blocks and first border.

¾ yd. gold lamé for some stars and 2nd border (this border will have to be pieced; if you want the side strips to be one piece, you will need 1¾ yds. and will have a lot left over).

Backing and batting larger than 45" x 45" finished size of the quilt.

## INSTRUCTIONS

•Some of these blocks are a little more complicated to piece than others. Some blocks were chosen from EQ2's ready-made libraries of star blocks rather than drawing them, although a few lines were changed on a couple of the blocks. There are several set-ins to piece in the blocks shown, so if you are new to working with template piecework, you might want to review construction techniques before you start working on the blocks with set-in seams.

•The numbers shown on the Electric Quilt block diagrams are not the order of piecing, but are just to show the different shapes in the blocks. EQ2 sees mirror-image shapes as two different templates, rather than just a reversal.

Eileen Thompson Lehner of Tyrone, PA, came to quiltmaking from the field of engineering, where she worked as an industrial project designer. A computer owner since 1984, her interest in 'the machine' is the focus for much of her quiltmaking. Eileen does technical support on Prodigy® for The Electric Quilt Company. Her AQS book, **Electronic Quilting**, is slated for publication in 1996, and will be a comprehensive workbook and reference for computerized quiltmakers.

Eileen Thompson Lehner

•For the outermost border of squares, which also serves as a fold-over binding, make strip-pieced units with strips that are rotary-cut 2" wide, sewn in graduated order of the colors used. The strips are then cut into 2½" segments, which is the width needed for a border that finishes to 1½" with enough extra to turn over to the back and hem for an edge finish. This takes the place of an applied binding.

•The dimensions of the borders are as follows: First border, hand-dyed fabric: strips cut 2½" wide, finished width 2"; Second border, gold tissue lamé: strips cut 1½" wide, finished width 1"; Outside (pieced border): strip-pieced cross-cut segments 2½" wide, finished width after turning over edge for binding, 1½".

Border #1 – 2" finished width – dyed fabric
Border #2 – 1" finished width – lamé
Border #3 – 1½" finished width – squares

•The overall finished dimensions of the quilt are 45" wide by 54" long. The size of the individual star blocks is 9" square. It is easier to press the seams open when constructing the blocks for this quilt rather than pressing them to one side, as it helps to minimize the seam thicknesses and make the machine quilting easier. Since it is to hang on a wall, pressed-open seams should not present a durability problem as compared to a quilt made for a bed. The quilt shown was machine quilted with gold metallic thread in a couple of decorative patterns, to give the effect of radiation outward from the large central star.

•Full size templates are provided for several of the stars. You can enlarge the remaining stars by using the grid method or enlarge on a photocopy machine to the 9" finished-size blocks.

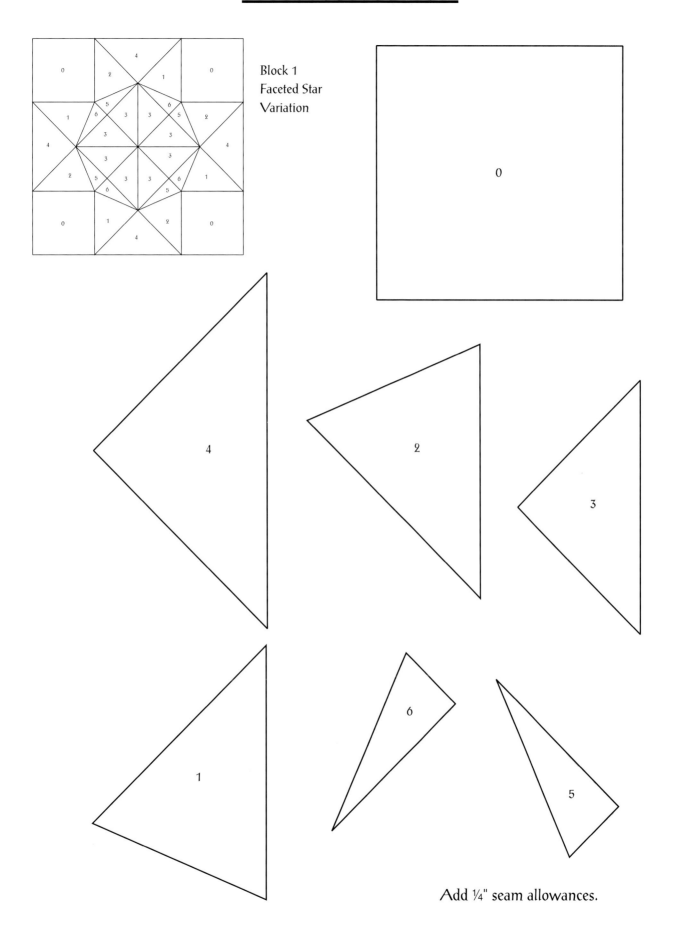

Block 1
Faceted Star
Variation

Add ¼" seam allowances.

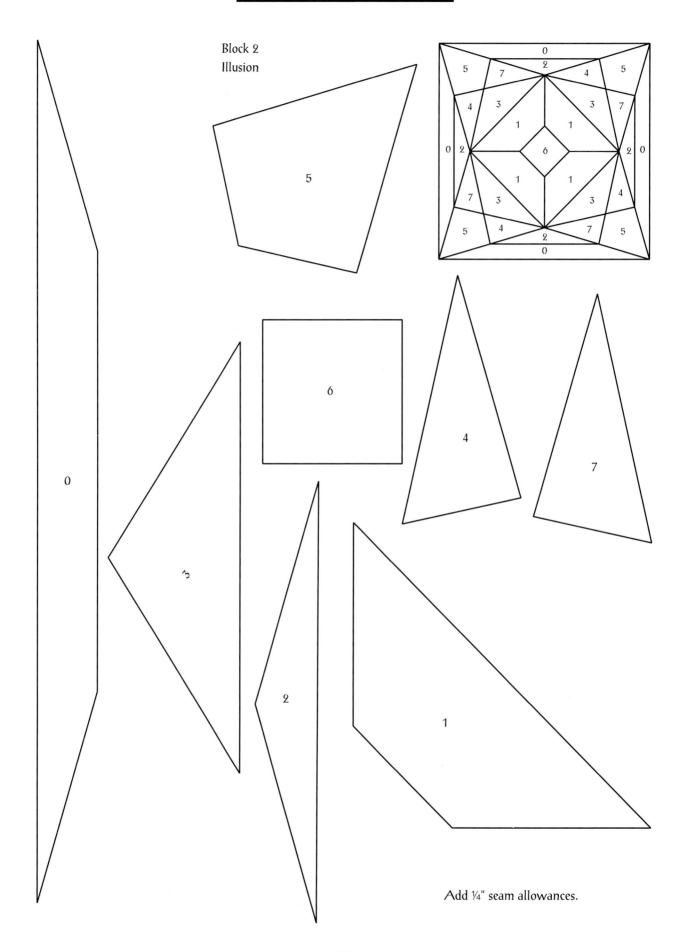

Block 2
Illusion

Add ¼" seam allowances.

# STARRY CHRISTMAS NIGHT

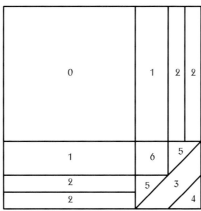

Block 6
Star of Bethlehem Variation

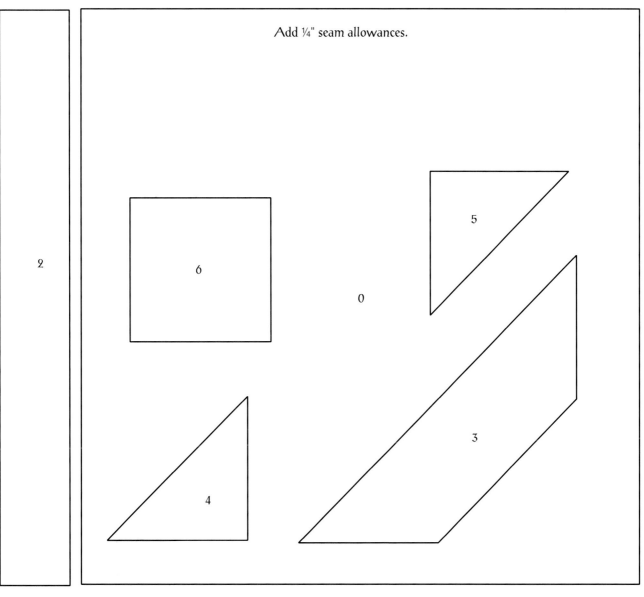

Add ¼" seam allowances.

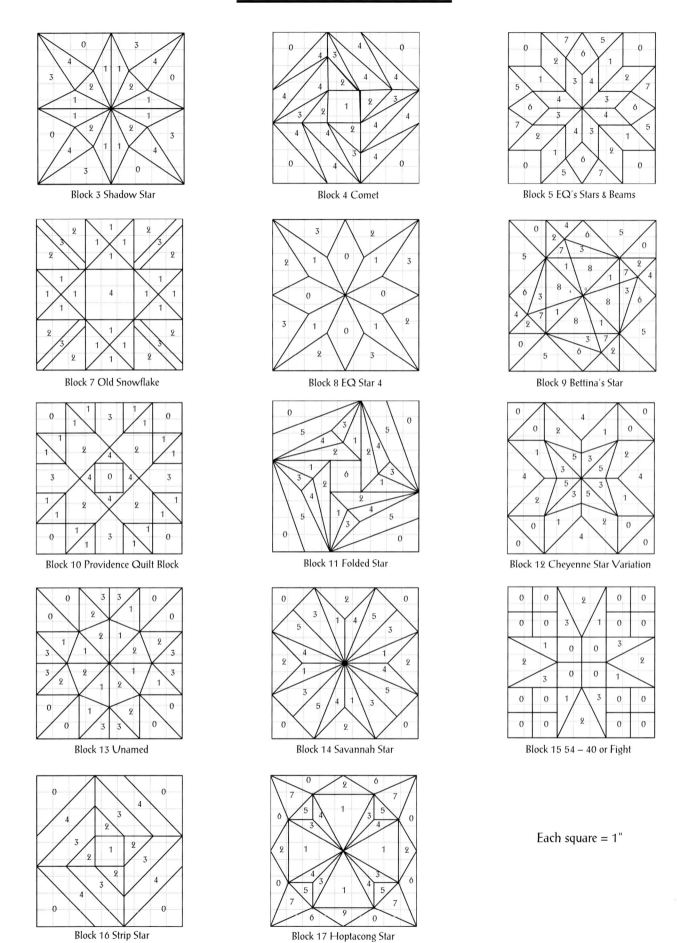

Block 3 Shadow Star

Block 4 Comet

Block 5 EQ's Stars & Beams

Block 7 Old Snowflake

Block 8 EQ Star 4

Block 9 Bettina's Star

Block 10 Providence Quilt Block

Block 11 Folded Star

Block 12 Cheyenne Star Variation

Block 13 Unamed

Block 14 Savannah Star

Block 15 54 – 40 or Fight

Block 16 Strip Star

Block 17 Hoptacong Star

Each square = 1"

# TABLE TOPPER

### by Dixie Haywood

This design uses under pressed-piecing on temporary foundations to make the piecing easy and precise. Size: 31" square.

**FEATURED TECHNIQUES**
Pressed piecing on foundation

## MATERIALS LIST

½ yard red print
¼ yard gold print
½ yard black print
1 obese-eighth (9" x 22"): green print
¼ yard white print
1 yard backing
Tracing paper or removable interfacing for temporary piecing foundation
Sewing machine
Basic sewing supplies

## INSTRUCTIONS

•Cut borders and corner triangles as follows: Red, cut two 12¼" squares diagonally to form 4 triangles; gold, cut four strips 1½" x 26"; black, cut four strips 3½" x 32".

•Prepare a master pattern. Draw an 8" square. Divide with diagonal lines into four triangular sections. Trace the pattern into each section, matching the lines of the pattern to complete the block.

•Prepare foundations. If using removable interfacing, trace the master pattern on four foundations. If using tracing paper, trace the pattern on one sheet. Layer with three more sheets of tracing paper and stitch through all layers with an unthreaded sewing machine. Trim paper to the outside edge of the patterns so that the foundation is the finished size of the block.

•Mark each foundation with the colors chosen for the star on the top of the foundation. (If you have needle-punched, this will be the smooth side of the paper.) Cut each foundation into the four triangular sections of the original pattern. Since the four foundation segments within each block are pieced with different colors, it is less confusing to piece all those using the same color before going on to the next color mix.

Dixie Haywood, Pensacola, FL, made her first quilt forty years ago. She didn't make another for fifteen years, but she hasn't stopped since! Dixie teaches and judges throughout the country and has authored over 150 articles and five books (three with Jane Hall). **Firm Foundations: Techniques and Quilt Blocks for Precision Piecing**, by Dixie and Jane Hall, will be published by AQS in 1996.

Dixie Haywood

•Cut the fabric for the pieced blocks using rough-cut templates. Trace the pattern pieces from the original foundation, marking the correct grain line. Lay each pattern on the wrong side of the fabric, maintaining the grain line, and cut with a ⅜" to ½" seam allowance.

•The pattern pieces are numbered in piecing order. Lay the wrong side of the patch #1 on the under side of the foundation, with ¼" seam allowance extending beyond the line between piece #1 and #2 and adequate seam allowance on the other sides. Pin in place. If you have needle-punched the foundations, the fabric will be wrong side against the rough side of the foundation; if using removable interfacing, the color notations will be on top and the fabric will be underneath.

•Lay patch #2 right side against patch #1, checking to be sure it will cover the foundation with ¼" seam allowance beyond the edge when sewn in place. Stitch on the marked line through all layers with 12 – 14 stitches to an inch. Trim the seam if it is in excess of ¼". Open patch #2 and press firmly from both sides of the

foundation, checking that there is no "pleat" at the seam. Pin in place.

•Fold back the foundation on the seam line between patch #1 and #3 and trim patch #1 to ¼" seam allowance before positioning patch #3 for stitching. Stitch, open, and press patch #3. Fold back the stitching line for patch #4 and trim as before. Stitch patch #4 in place. As each foundation is covered, press firmly. Leaving ¼" seam allowance beyond the foundation on all sides, trim any excess fabric.

•Lay out the four segments for each block to match the colors. Pin, matching points and the edge of the foundations. Stitch, using the foundation edge as a sewing guide. Press open the seams for the most accurate match.

•Construct the quilt according to the layout. After the corner triangles are sewn around the four-block center, true up the edges leaving ¼" seam allowance, before adding the borders.

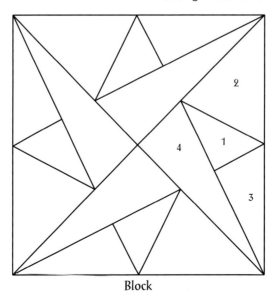

Block

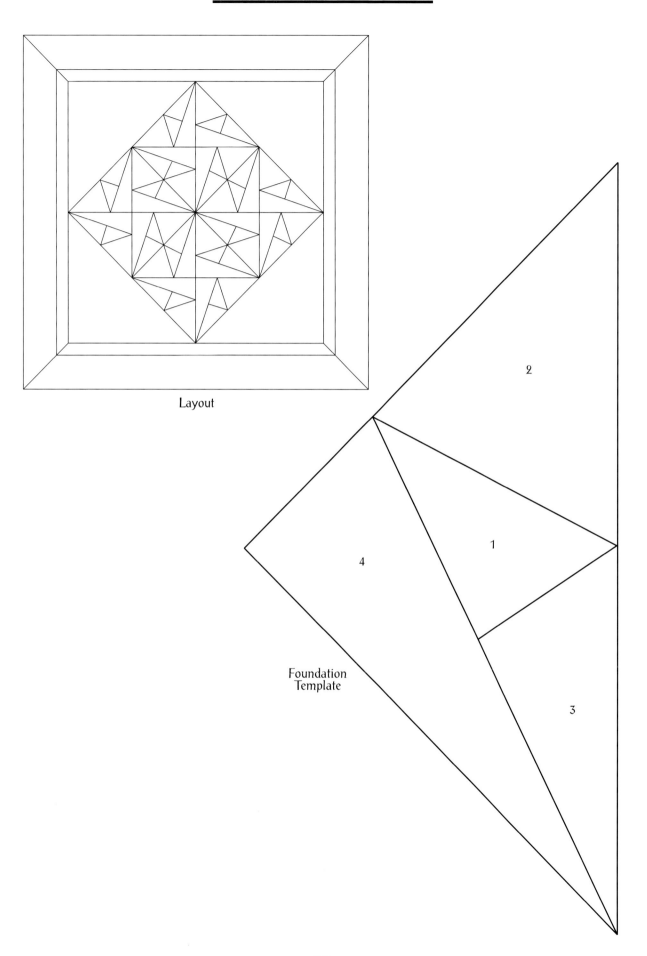

Layout

Foundation
Template

2

1

4

3

# SURPRISE PACKAGE
## WALLHANGING

by Patricia B. Campbell

Everyone loves surprise packages. The inspiration for this little wallhanging came from an exquisitely wrapped gift to Patricia from her husband. What wonderful surprises were inside! Surprise Package was hand quilted by Michelle L. Jack.

## FEATURED TECHNIQUES
## Appliqué

## MATERIALS LIST

1 fat quarter for center (background)
1 fat quarter for inner border
1 fat quarter for outer border and binding
¼ yd. for backing and sleeve
A colorful assortment of fabrics for your packages, tulips, leaves, and ribbons
Template material, pins, needles, thimble, marking pencils, scissors
Thread to match appliqué fabrics
Quilting thread
Batting
Binding – ¼" finished

## INSTRUCTIONS

•Keep your fat quarter background fabric intact for

hand stitching. You can cut and square up after you have completed your appliqué.

•Remember to add ¼" seam allowance to your background and border pieces. Add ⅛" seam allowance to all appliqué pieces, and cut 1¼" strips for binding. A 3" (finished) rod pocket sleeve (for hanging) was added to the backing.

•Trace the pattern onto your background fabric, marking a little inside of each piece, so you're not troubled with having to cover those marked lines. Or, don't mark at all, just center the packages on the background fabric and place the flowers and leaves randomly for a carefree experience.

•Use your favorite method of hand or machine appliqué. "Surprise Package" was made entirely by

Patricia Campbell, Dallas, TX, is an internationally-recognized quilt artist, teacher, lecturer, and author. She adapts antique Jacobean embroidery designs to contemporary hand appliqué. Pat has exhibited her quilts in shows across the U.S., winning numerous awards for her works of art. She is the co-author with Mimi Ayars of four books including **Jacobean Appliqué Book I: "Exotica,"** AQS, and **Jacobean Appliqué Book II: "Romantica"** to be released by AQS in the fall of 1995.

Patricia B. Campbell

hand, using the needle turn method. You decide. . .it can be done with freezer paper, blanket stitching the raw edges, iron-on fusible material, invisible machine stitching, or your favorite technique.

"Surprise Package" was hand quilted with variegated metallic thread. All flowers, leaves, and ribbons were shadow quilted ⅛" to ¼" out from the designs, and star shapes were placed randomly in the background.

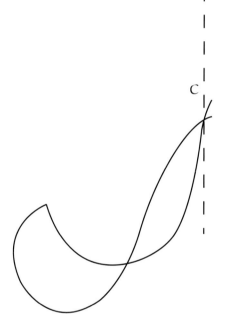

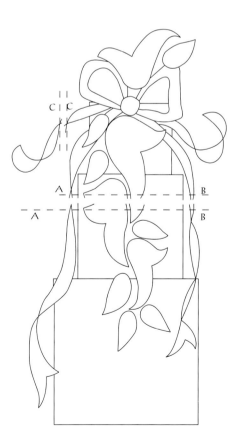

A

B

# THESE TREES COME DECORATED
## WALLHANGING

**by Klaudeen Hansen**

It won't take anytime at all to decorate these trees. By choosing colorful red and green prints with glittery gold outlines, the trees will be decorated as soon as they are stitched. Five Log Cabin style tree blocks and two borders are combined to make this charming 26" square wallhanging.

## FEATURED TECHNIQUES
### Machine pieced Log Cabin style tree

## MATERIALS LIST

⅞ yd. light "snowy" background
⅛ yd. each, 5 different green Christmas prints
⅛ yd. solid green for trunks & inner border
¼ yd. Christmas print for outer border
⅛ yd. for binding (can be same as border)

## CUTTING

**Background "snowy" fabric**
1 – 12" square, cut with an "X" for side triangles
2 – 7" squares, cut once diagonally for corners
5 – 4" squares, cut once diagonally
3 – 1½" strips, can be 44" strips or more shorter strips; from one strip, cut 10 – 1½" pieces and 10 – 2½" pieces.

**Trees**
One strip 1½" x 44" of each of your 5 greens
One strip 1¼" x 44" of trunk fabric, cut into 5 pieces

5 squares 2½" x 2½" ground fabric

**Border**
2 – 1¼" strips of tree trunk fabric for inner border
2 – 3½" strips of Christmas print for outer border

## INSTRUCTIONS

**Tree trunk**
•Cut the five 4" squares of background fabric in half diagonally. Sew trunk fabric to each side of the diagonal cut edge. Press seams under trunk (Figure 1). Cut this down to a 3½" square, keeping the trunk fabric centered. Iron the 5 squares (2½") of ground fabric in half

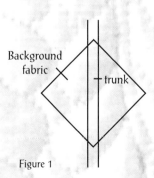

Figure 1

Klaudeen Hansen, Sun Prairie, WI, is a well-known teacher and judge, who has judged more than 12,100 quilts at shows and state fairs across the country. She is chairman of the international AQS Quilt Competition in Paducah, KY, and since 1985 has been co-editor of the **Quilt Art Engagement Calendar**, an AQS bestseller. Some of her Amish style quilts are displayed at the American Embassy, Oslo, Norway.

Klaudeen Hansen

diagonally. Unfold square and place it right sides together to one trunk corner, with ironed crease going across trunk. Stitch on ironed line. Trim ¼" seam allowance, (Figure 2). After cutting, press remaining triangle down to complete the square tree trunk unit.

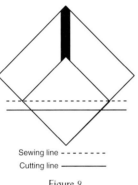

Sewing line - - - - - - - -
Cutting line ————

Figure 2

## Making tree, using Log Cabin method
•See the Assembly Diagram. The branches are numbered in the order they are to be stitched; #7 & #8 are background fabric.

•Sew green strip tree branch across top on left side, trim even with trunk section; then add green strip to right side and trim. Press all seams toward outside edge of block.

•Sew 1½" square of light background to each end of green strips #3 and #4. Press seams under dark fabric. Stitch to both left and right side of tree.

•Sew 1½" x 2½" light background to both ends of green strips #5 and #6. Stitch to both left and right sides of tree.

•Sew light background strips #7 and #8 to both left and right side of tree. Press and square trees to same size (approx. 7½").

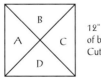

12" square of background. Cut with an "X."

Figure 3

## Completing wallhanging
•Lay out trees on diagonal. Fill in corners and side triangles with light

7" squares of background. Cut once diagonally.

background fabric, cut as shown in Figure 3. Sew block and triangles in diagonal rows. Sew rows together and square all edges and corners. See Assembly Diagram.

•Inner border strips are cut 1¼" wide. Outer border strips are cut 3½" wide. Each border is sewn to the top first, then both sides, with the bottom last. Be sure to measure sides and make them equal so your quilt will be straight.

•Layer with backing and batting and secure with pins before quilting by hand or machine. Trim edges and square corners before binding with French fold binding.

Assembly Diagram

# *Victorian Hospitality*

## PINEAPPLE LOG CABIN WALL QUILT

### by Barbara Ann Caron

The pineapple motif has long been a symbol of hospitality and may be found in decorative arts and furnishings. At the same time, the Pineapple Log Cabin variation is visually interesting, with its combination of radial and concentric rhythms. This 22" x 22" decorative quilt combines the symbolism of hospitality – which is so appropriate for the holidays – with foundation piecing, Victorian tucked logs, and the colors of Christmas.

## FEATURED TECHNIQUES
Tucked Pineapple Log Cabin blocks
with foundation piecing

Although not unique to the United States, the Log Cabin quilt achieved its greatest popularity here. The Log Cabin quilt, a member of the "pressed quilt" family, was constructed using foundation blocks. The center square was positioned on the foundation and the "logs" were added in a specific order. After each log was sewn, the fabric was folded back and pressed in place prior to attaching the next log. Frequently, Log Cabin quilts were tied rather than quilted. For hundreds of years, quiltmakers were attracted to the Log Cabin quilt for both its beauty and its simplicity of construction. Through the phases and fads in quiltmaking, it was always in vogue. However, during the Victorian period, beginning around 1880, more ornate quilts became fashionable. Rather than put aside the Log Cabin design, some quiltmakers modified it slightly with the addition of a decorative tuck or fold along the length of

the logs. This embellishment adds a soft, dimensional quality to the quilt. The Pineapple variation of the traditional Log Cabin block has a special cultural and aesthetic appeal.

## MATERIALS LIST

⅛ yard red print or enough for nine 2" squares
¾ yard cream print
1½ yards green print #1 for logs, borders, backing, and binding
½ yard green print #2
1 yard muslin for foundation squares and border interfacing

All fabrics should be at least 42" wide, 100% cotton, pre-washed, and pressed.

Barbara Ann Caron has been a quiltmaker since 1976, and is the author of **Tessellations & Variations: Creating One-Patch and Two-Patch Quilts**, AQS. She offers a wide variety of classes on quilt design and techniques. Barbara also teaches design at the University of Northern Iowa, Cedar Falls, IA. This project is an outgrowth of her interest in 19th century design.

Barbara Ann Caron

## CUTTING

•This quilt is easy to assemble, but requires accuracy in cutting the strips. A rotary cutter is recommended. Seam allowances have been included. Refer to Figure 1 as needed.

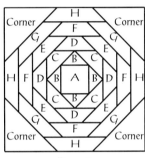

Figure 1

•From the red print, cut nine 2" squares, for center square A.

•From the cream print, cut 12 strips that are 1½" wide and the full width of the fabric. From these strips, cut a total of 36 logs in each of the following lengths: 2" for B, 2½" for D, 3" for F, and 3½" for H.

| 6" x 16" | 6" x 16" | 6" x 16" | 4" x 22" | |
|---|---|---|---|---|
| | | | 4" x 22" Top and bottom border strips | |
| Center backing strips | | | 4" x 22" | |
| | | | 4" x 22" | |
| 4" x 16" | 4" x 16" | Front and back side borders 4" x 16" | 4" x 16" | 2" x 26" |
| | | | | 2" x 26" Binding strips |
| | | | | 2" x 26" |
| | | | | 2" x 26" |

Figure 2
Green print #1 cutting guide

•From the green print #1, cut six strips that are 1½" wide and the full width of the fabric. From these strips, cut a total of 36 logs in each of the following lengths: 2½" for C and 3½" for G. Also cut the border, backing, and binding strips from this fabric. See Figure 2 for the quantity and dimensions.

•From the green print #2, cut three strips that are 1½"

wide and the full width of the fabric. From these strips, cut a total of 36 logs that are each 3" long for E. Then, cut three strips that are 2⅞" wide. From these strips, cut 36 corner triangles, using the corner cutting template (Figure 3, pg. 144). The grainline marking on the template must match the straight grain of the fabric. This triangle is slightly oversized and will be trimmed to the final size after the block is pieced.

| Interfacing for front/back side borders | | | | Interfacing for top/bottom borders | | |
|---|---|---|---|---|---|---|
| 4" x 16" | 4" x 16" | 4" x 16" | 4" x 16" | 4" x 22" | | |
| | | | | 4" x 22" | | |
| | | | | 4" x 22" | | |
| | | | | 4" x 22" | | |
| 8" x 8" Foundation blocks | 8" x 8" | 8" x 8" | 8" x 8" | 8" x 8" | | |
| 8" x 8" | 8" x 8" | 8" x 8" | 8" x 8" | | | |

Figure 4
Muslin cutting guide

•From the muslin, cut nine foundation squares as well as fabric to "interface" the borders. This is necessary so the weight of the borders is the same as the height of the center of the quilt. See Figure 4 for the quantity and dimensions.

## MARKING

•This step must be executed with careful attention to accuracy, so that all logs finish to a consistent ½" width.

•In preparation for piecing, tape the 6" marking grid (Figure 5, pg. 145) to a light box. One at a time, center the 8" foundation squares over the grid, taping them in place. (The excess foundation fabric will be trimmed away after the block is pieced.) Using a ruler and sharp pencil, accurately transfer all the grid lines to the foundation square. The lines should be light, but easily visible. To avoid missing lines, follow a consistent order: horizontal, vertical, diagonal, and diagonal.

•Double check to make certain all lines have been transferred. Remove the foundation square and set it aside for piecing.

## PIECING

•A fabric foundation piecing technique is used. That is, logs are aligned, sewn with a ¼" seam allowance, folded back to the pencil line, and pressed in place. (Notice that the pencil line is not the stitching line, but the location of the raw edge of the fabric). Because the logs are ½" wider than the space between the grid lines, the excess fabric results in a ¼" tuck along the length of each log.

---

### SPECIAL TIPS
•Organize all of the pieces in order from A to H and the corner triangle. Always center the logs. Sometimes they extend from grid line to grid line and sometimes they fall between grid lines. Use cream or white thread so the stitching lines do not show through if a light value backing fabric is used. Do not backstitch when attaching the logs. This will facilitate trimming away the excess fabric tails as additional logs are attached. Always trim fabric tails and thread ends so the front and back side of the block are both neat. Grade all seam allowances that "shadow" through the light value logs. Press often.

---

•Place the red print square (A) in the center of the foundation block (Figure 6).

•Position two B logs (cream print), so the raw edges line up with the top and bottom of the center square. Stitch the

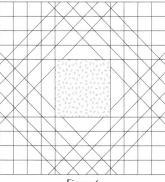
Figure 6

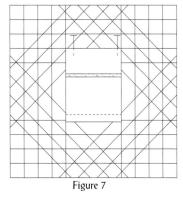
Figure 7

logs in place and then fold them back to the next pencil line, making certain that there is a tuck in each log (Figure 7). Position the second pair of B logs at the sides. Sew and press in place.

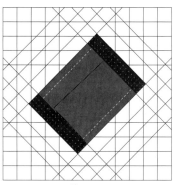
Figure 8

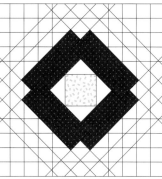
Figure 9

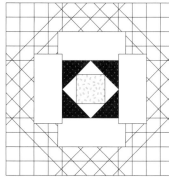
Figure 10

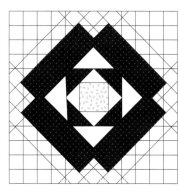
Figure 11

•Following the same procedure, position and sew the C logs (green print #1). Trim away the excess tails of the B logs (Figure 8). Fold the C logs back to the next diagonal pencil line, making certain that there is a tuck in each log. The center square is now surrounded by light triangles (Figure 9). NOTE: In the finished block, only the B logs have a triangle shape. All other logs are trapezoids, although this does not become apparent until the E logs are added.

•Continuing the procedure, position and sew the D logs (cream print). Trim

away the excess tails of C logs. Fold the logs back to the next pencil line, making certain that there is a tuck in each log (Figure 10).

•Continue alternating the green (E and G logs) and the cream (F and H) logs, carefully centering, sewing, trimming, and pressing. From this point onward, it should be possible to attach all four logs at the same time, rather than working in pairs. Notice that, with the attachment of the E logs, the C through H logs begin to take on their final trapezoid shape (Figure 11).

•To complete the block, attach the corner triangles, centering them carefully. Sew and trim. From an index card, make a copy of the corner pressing template (Figure 12, pg. 144). Then, to insure that all the corners are exactly the same size, position this pressing template at the corner of the foundation grid lines. Fold the triangle of fabric over the template and press (Figure 13).

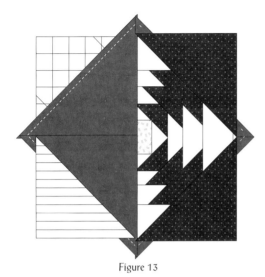

Figure 13

•Trim away the excess foundation block and triangle fabric. The block is now a 6" square (Figure 14). Assemble the remaining eight blocks in the same manner.

Figure 14

## SETTING

•Use a ½" seam allowance to sew the blocks together and attach the borders. This compensates for the lack of a ¼" tuck between adjacent blocks and between blocks and borders. Use a thread color that matches the darkest fabric.

•Sew the blocks together to create three separate vertical strips of three blocks each, taking care to match the edges of the corner triangles. Press the seam allowances to one side – in alternate directions on each strip of blocks. To reduce bulk, grade the underneath seam allowances to ¼". Each strip measures 6" x 16".

•Using a quilt-as-you-go (or sew-and-flip) assembly technique, back the center strip of blocks with one of the 6" x 16" strips of backing fabric. Wrong sides of the fabric are together. Pin the edges.

•Attach a strip of blocks to one side of the center. That is, place the right side of the second strip of blocks to the right side of the center strip of blocks. Then, place the right side of the second strip of backing fabric to the right side of the center backing fabric. One raw edge of the center strip will be sandwiched between the top and backing of the strip being added. Sew a ½" seam allowance. Grade away the seam allowances closest to the backing fabric. Fold the fabrics out, enclosing the seam. Press.

•Repeat the previous step to attach the strip of blocks to the other side of the center strip. This nine-block center square measures 16" x 16".

•To give the borders the same weight as the center of the quilt, "interface" both the front and back border strips with a layer of muslin. The muslin may be pinned or basted in place for ease of assembly.

•Attach the side borders first, using the same method as for joining the strips of blocks, including a ½" seam allowance.

•Attach the top and bottom borders, using the same method. The quilt now measures 22" square. If necessary, the corners may be squared up at this time.

## FINISHING

•Binding: A double binding, cut on the cross grain, is used to finish the quilt.

•Attach the strips of 2" wide binding fabric to each other to form a continuous strip of fabric that is approximately 96" long. Press wrong sides together lengthwise to make a 1" wide double binding.

•Using a ¼" seam allowance, apply the binding to the quilt, mitering at the corners. Fold the binding to cover the seam allowance and stitch it in place using small blind stitches. Remember to sew the miters closed.

•Quilting is not necessary. However, the quilt may be embellished with hand or machine stitches using cotton or metallic quilting thread.

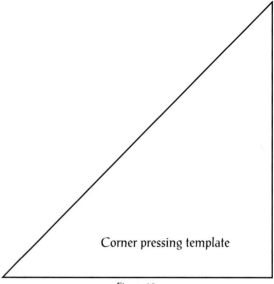

Corner pressing template

Figure 12

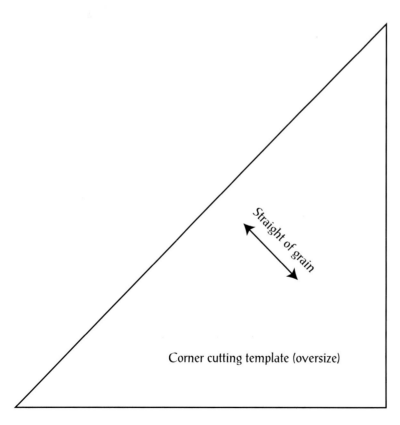

Straight of grain

Corner cutting template (oversize)

Figure 3

Figure 5

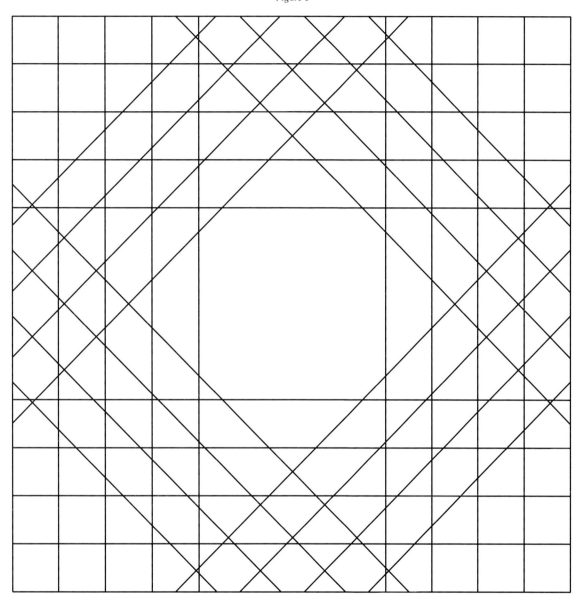

# 𝒱ICTORIAN 𝒮PLENDOR
## WALLHANGING

### by Barbara Barber

Everyone can imagine the old Victorian house, with the tree all decorated and snow covering the ground. Barbara Barber's pattern for Victorian Splendor will help you make your own Victorian wallhanging. Fusible appliqué will help you complete several for gifts too.

## FEATURED TECHNIQUES
## Fusible appliqué

## MATERIALS LIST

½ yd. house fabric
¼ yd. roof
¾ yd. sky
¼ yd. snow
½ – 1 yd. flowered (takes quite a bit to cut/match as a frame)
½ yd. trim/binding
**Scrap**:

       solid black (window base)
       chimney
       stained glass window fabric (small paisley)
3 yds. fusible web
1 yd. backing
1 yd. fleece
White paint with fabric writer tip, for icicles (white iridescent)

## LACE

1 yd. Victorian trim
1 yd. curtains (note medallion pattern)
1 yd. roof trim
¼ yd. porch railing

## EQUIPMENT

See-thru ruler with increment markings
Fine tip felt-tip pen for marking fusible web
Small, sharp pointed scissors
Rotary cutter and mat
6" see-thru ruler is helpful

Barbara Barber is a quiltmaker, lecturer, and teacher, who enjoys every phase of quilt-making, from long-term broderie perse pieces to quick, fusible appliqué projects, such as "Victorian Splendor." Quilting is an art form stimulated by past generations and it provides Barbara the opportunities to draw upon those roots; to become more adventuresome; to experiment with new techniques; to take new directions. Her book on broderie perse will be published by AQS.

Barbara Barber

## BUILDING TIPS

•When working with fusible web, assymetrical designs must be drawn mirror image of final result. In Victorian house only the 2 ell roofs/snow/trim, fit this category. The rest of the design is reversible. Notice that the patterns are drawn reverse image so you can trace directly onto the fusible web paper, iron web to the back of your fabric and house will appear as in color photo.

•Just as in traditional appliqué, parts of the design that are recessed must have allowance enough to underlay its neighbor.

•When building your house, start from the furthest away parts and work forward.

•Sometimes it is advantageous to build onto a base fabric, and in this case the house proper is so constructed. Draw house outline (no turrets/chimneys) onto fusible web, reverse image and press to house fabric. Cut out whole house and leave paper on. Trace front of Victorian house, outline only. Press to house fabric and leave paper on.

## INSTRUCTIONS

### Windows
•Trace entire window shape onto fusible web. Do all windows, press enmasse onto black, cut out individual windows and leave paper on. Trace outside window, trim onto fusible web, do all windows. Allow enough for cross pieces. Note difference in width of cross pieces on different windows. Press enmasse onto trim color. Cut out of fusible web a strip of paisley (stained glass).

•Position lace on black. Press on with adhesive only. Protect iron with fusible web paper. Main window – insert tree.

•Insert paisley.

•Add crosspiece.

•Add window trim, build door likewise.

•Remove paper backing on windows/door, just before pressing to house.

•Build house in numbered sequence. Always positioning a bit ahead before pressing. NOTE: Ell roofs, #3's, snow, 9's, trim, #6's and #8's, are traced mirror images.

### Background
•Snow cut 9" x 25", sky cut 20" x 25", piece and press. To adhere house to background: assemble, position chimneys/turrets, and press. Check pattern for placement. Press house in place then add peak trim. Press from back also. Press with damp cloth as fusible web directs. Add shrubs and wreath. Square piece up.

**Borders:** Fusible web print, cut, position, press, and damp press. If drawing lettering on backing, do so before layering then layer, quilt, bind, and add circles. Hot glue bow to wreath. Did you really think I sewed it on? Add a narrow sleeve for rod and sign work. Make a cup of strong tea – sit back and admire your handwork!

NOTE: Front section of my house was constructed with layers of scalloped strips, but the effect was not worth the trouble.

Smoke

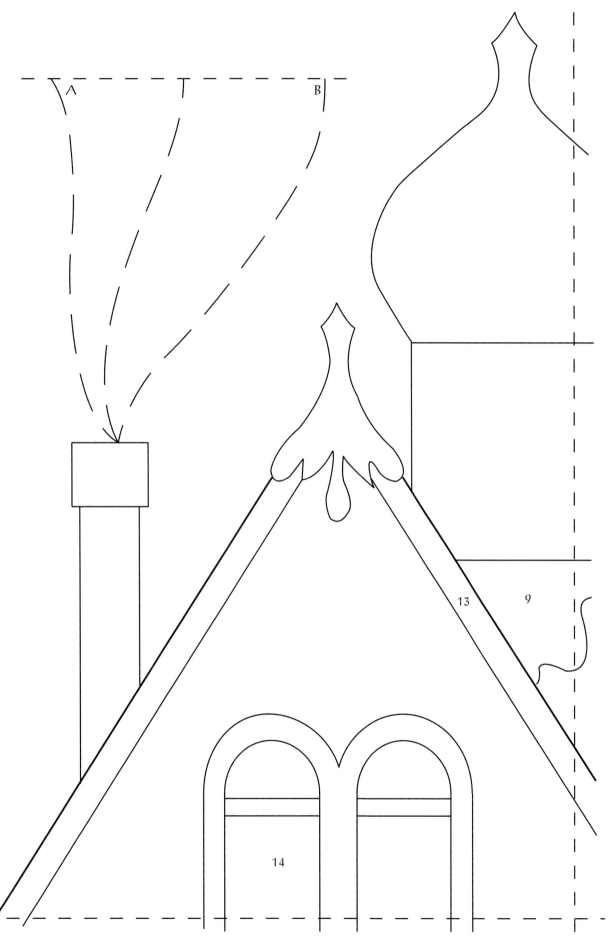

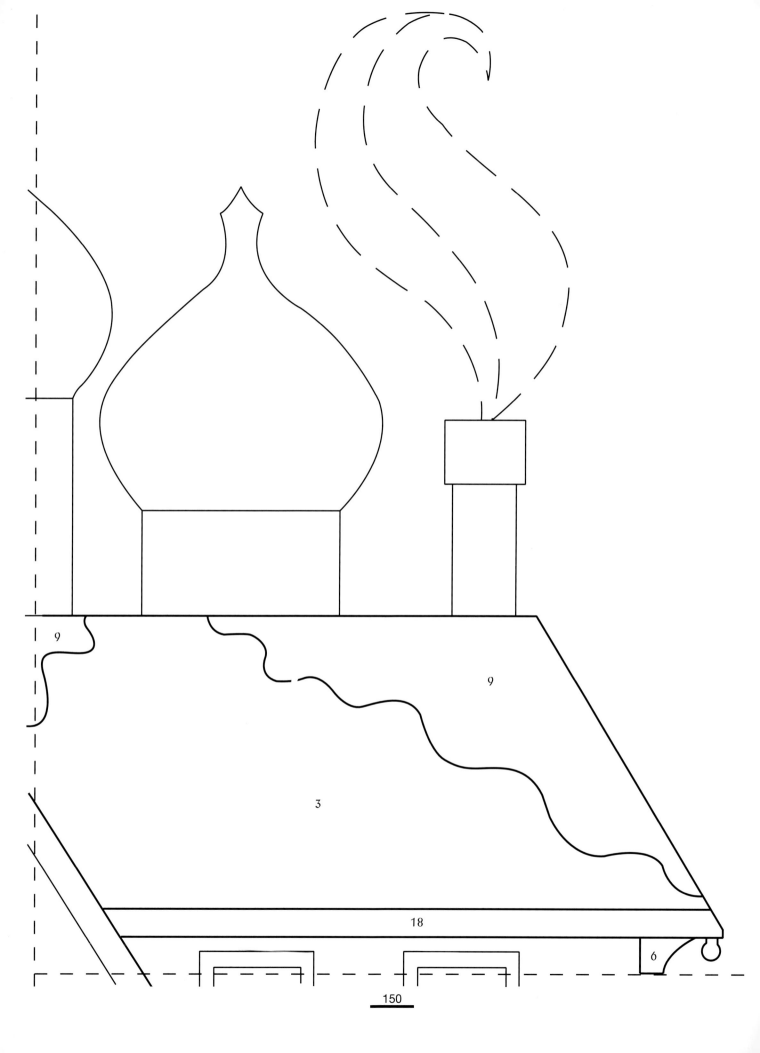

9

9

3

18

6

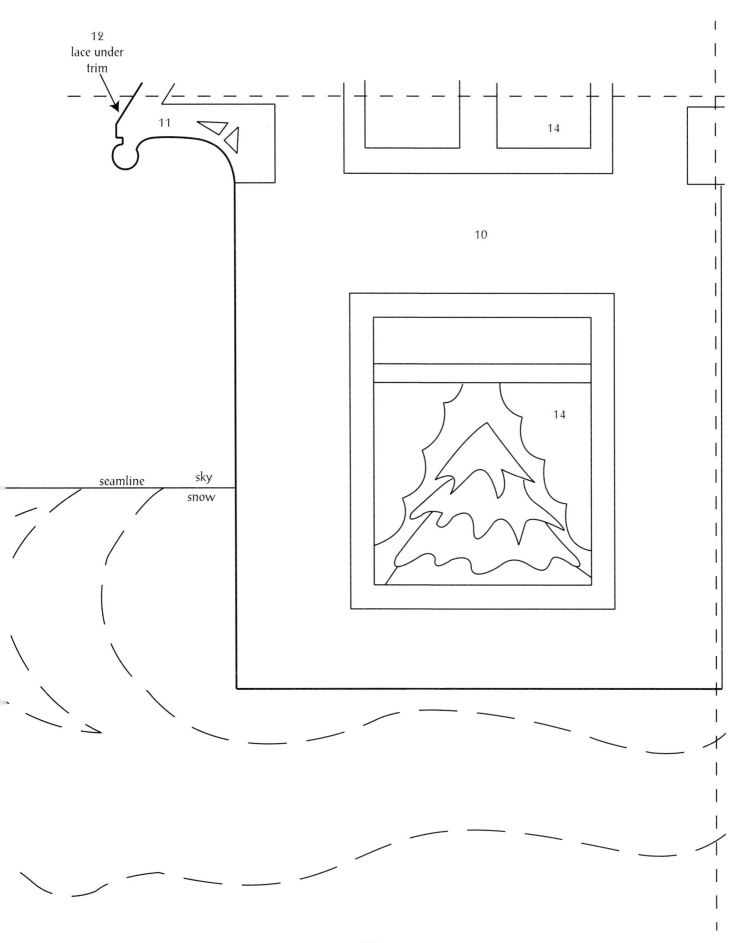

12
lace under
trim

11

14

10

14

seamline

sky

snow

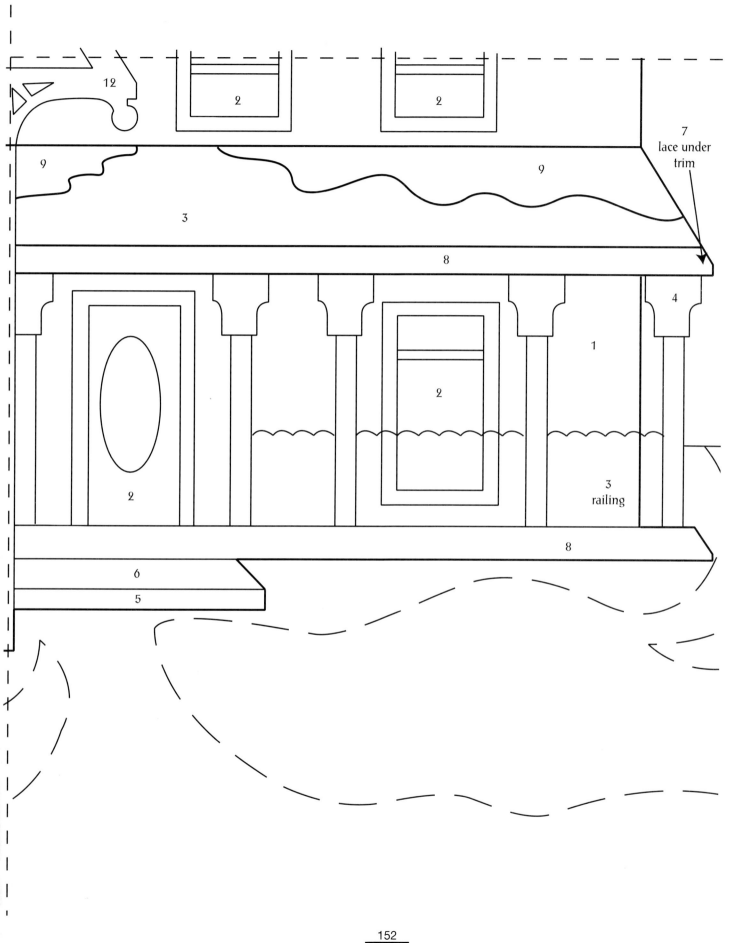

# WHOLE CLOTH STOCKING

**by Bettina Havig**

When it's time to hang your stocking by the chimney with care, this whole cloth Christmas stocking is a perfect choice. The stocking is made of cotton sateen and hand quilted. The lining is a festive Christmas plaid with a woven gold thread. The finished stocking is approximately 18" long.

## FEATURED TECHNIQUES
### Whole cloth quilting

## MATERIALS LIST

½ yard forest green cotton sateen or solid color fabric of your choice
½ yard muslin for backing/lining of quilting
¾ yard plaid for stocking inner lining and cuff
20" x 40" batting, low loft preferable
¼ yard matching grosgrain ribbon, ⅜" wide or ¼ yard gold cord
Optional: 2 – 3 jingle bells
Thread to match the stocking color – need not be quilting thread

## INSTRUCTIONS

•Trace quilting design onto the front of your stocking,

dark fabric may require the use of a light table or light source. Use a marker which you have pretested for removability and yet is visible for quilting. Make sure that you outline the shape of the stocking. Do not cut the stocking out – leave your fabric in a rectangle so that it will be easier to handle while quilting. Baste the stocking front, batting, and lining together. Hand quilt using matching thread. Reverse the direction of the pattern and trace only the background pattern onto the back of the stocking. Do not cut out the stocking shape. Baste the back, batt, and lining. Hand quilt using matching thread.

**Inner lining and cuff**
•Cut two pieces of lining, right sides facing by using the stocking shape pattern, allow ½" seam allowance. Cut cuff from cuff pattern. Join front and back of lining, leav-

Bettina Havig, Columbia, MO, has been quilting since 1970, teaching since 1974, and owned a quilt shop from 1977 to 1985. She is a quiltmaker, teacher, lecturer, judge, quilt historian, and consultant, who has been on the program of symposia and guilds across the country and abroad. She is co-curator of a special exhibition of Amish crib quilts from the collection of Sara Miller at MAQS in the summer of 1996.

Bettina Havig

ing open between marks. Join cuff front and back. Sew cuff to top of lining, matching at side seams. The opposite edge is to be sewn to the quilted stocking in the final step.

### Finishing the stocking and lining
•Trim quilted stocking sections to shape (allowing ½" seam allowance). Baste outline of the stocking on both front and back of stocking as a guide for construction. Trim as much of batting as possible beyond the basted outline in order to reduce bulk in the seam. With right sides of stocking sections facing, stitch around stocking, leaving the top open. Turn stocking right side out. Clip curves only if necessary. Make sure that the inner lining is wrong side out and slip the quilted stocking into the lining. Stitch cuff edge to the top of the stocking opening. Pull stocking through the open space left in the lining and close the seam. Turn lining into the inside of stocking. Turn down cuff. Stitch ribbon or cord loop to left side seam top of stocking as it faces you. Embellish with jingle bells, if desired.

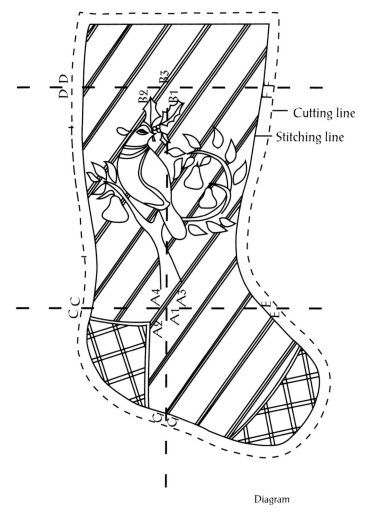

Cutting line
Stitching line

Diagram

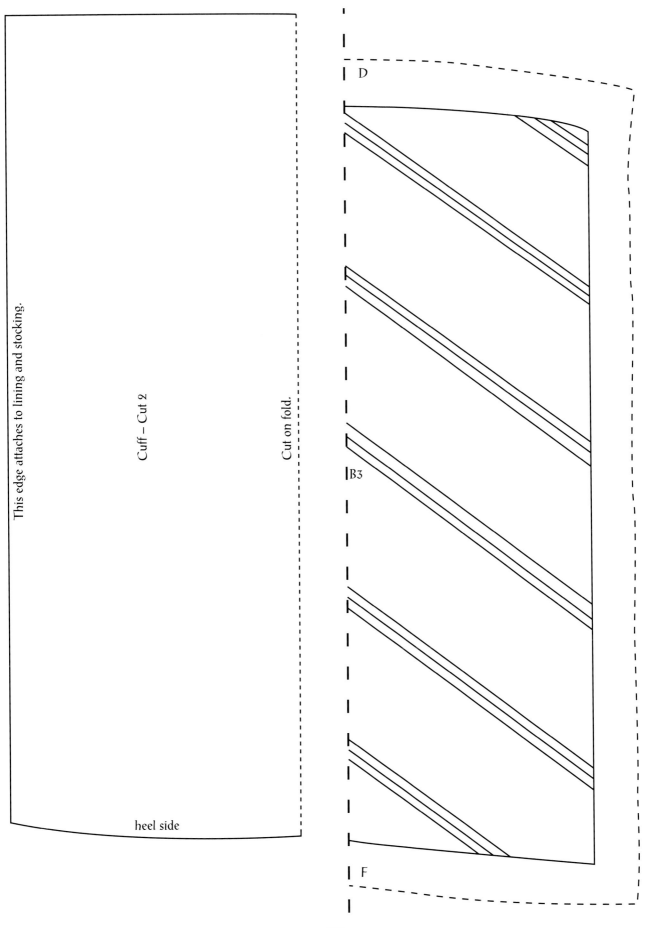

This edge attaches to lining and stocking.

Cuff – Cut 2

Cut on fold.

heel side

D

B3

F

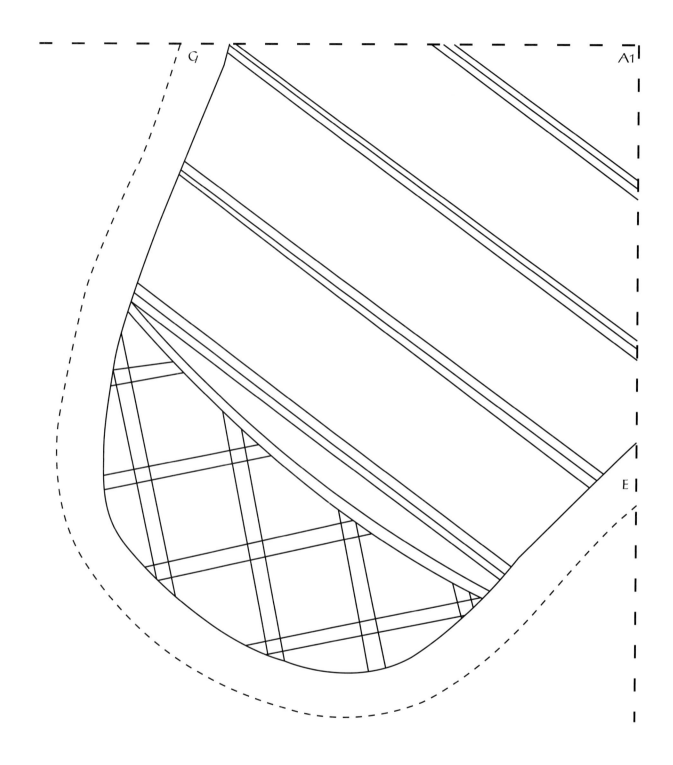

G

A1

E

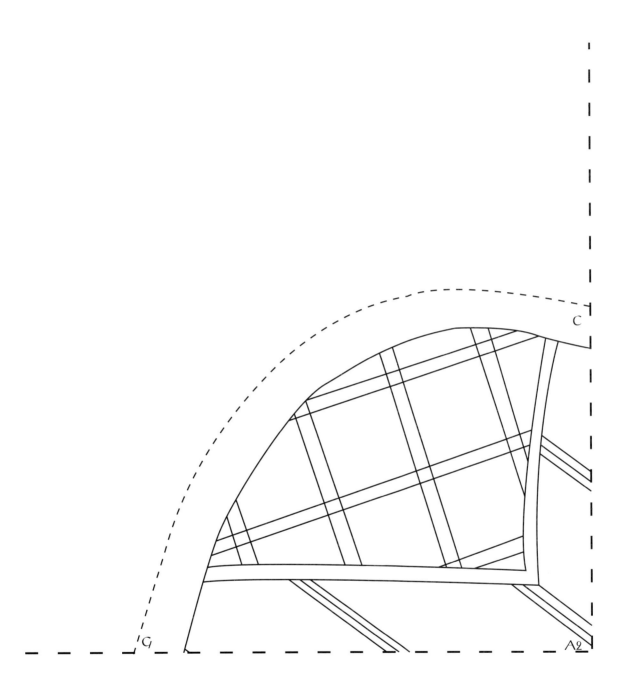

C

G                                A2

B1

F

A3

E

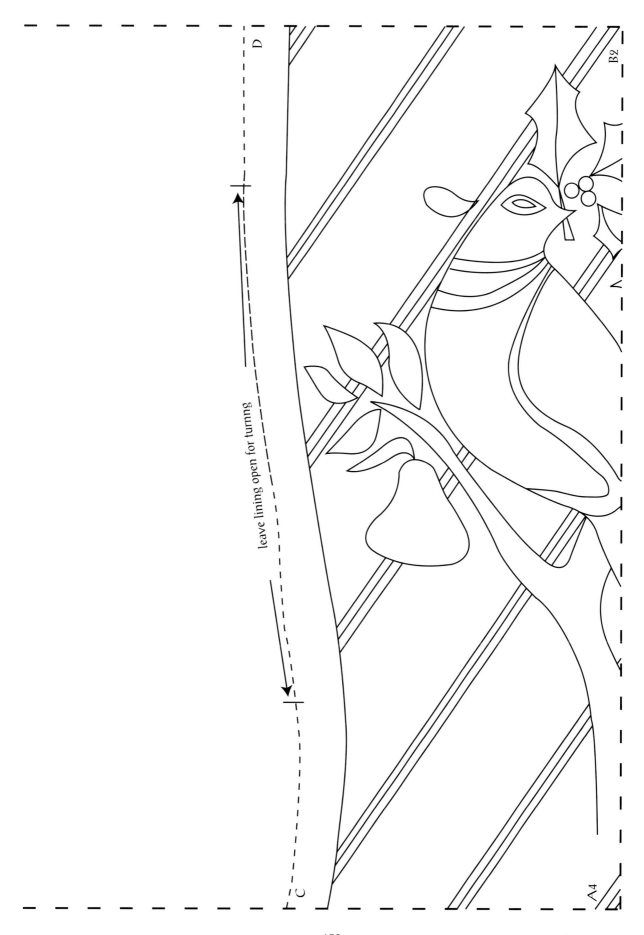

leave lining open for turning

# ⨳ American Quilter's Society ⨳
## dedicated to publishing books for today's quilters

*These books can be found in local bookstores and quilt shops. If you are unable to locate a title in your area, you can order by mail from AQS, P.O. Box 3290, Paducah, KY 42002-3290. Please add $2 for the first book and 40¢ for each additional one to cover postage and handling. (International orders please add $2.50 for the first book and $1 for each additional one.)*